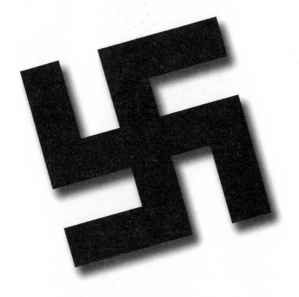

DRAGONS OF GOD

And we are here as on a darkling plain
Swept with confused alarms of struggle and flight,
Where ignorant armies clash by night.

Matthew Arnold, "Dover Beach"

DRAGONS OF GOD

A JOURNEY THROUGH FAR-RIGHT AMERICA

Vincent Coppola

LONGSTREET PRESS, INC.
Atlanta, Georgia

Published by Longstreet Press, Inc.
A subsidiary of Cox Newspapers,
A subsidiary of Cox Enterprises, Inc.
2140 Newmarket Parkway
Suite 118
Marietta, GA 30067

Printed in the United States of America
1st printing 1996
Library of Congress Catalog Card Number: 96-76508
ISBN 1-56352-327-2

Jacket and book design by Neil Hollingsworth

Dedication

For my parents, Gloria and Joe, and brother Tom whom I miss with every breath . . . my brothers, Joe and Greg, who chose life . . . my children, Gabrielle and Thomas, who sustain it.

— October 1996

Acknowledgments

I want to thank John Yow and Chuck Perry at Longstreet Press for providing the encouragement and support that made *Dragons* a reality. I want to thank my magnificent friends — Mike Dowling, Mary Farmer, Linda Peek, Mike Schact, John and Loretta McDonagh, Sal "Butch" and Rosemary Mulia, Bruno and Mayes Rubeo, Ben Pettinato (a good father), Robert Morris, Christianne Lauterbach, Tom and Janet Junod, Gina Picallo, Renee Kaswan, Lee Ann Broussard, Gus Kaufman, Bobby Vasquez, Margaret and Graham Anthony, Jane Kimbrell, Lee Walburn, and Emma Edmunds.

I want to thank the most loyal and gracious woman, Mary Lyon Jarman, for all her many kindnesses, and Melita Hayes for her years of support and understanding.

. . . and Meg Reggie, who makes me stronger

. . . and the kids, Katie and Drew, Thomas and Gaby, Rudy and Regina

. . . and that paragon of friendship, fellowship, and crusty pizza, Bob "Rocky" Russo.

Contents

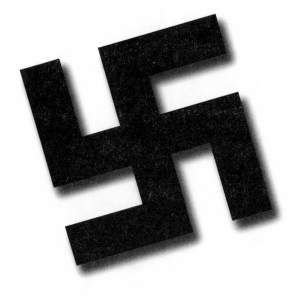

DRAGONS OF GOD

Think not that I am come to bring peace on earth. I came not to bring peace but a sword.

Jesus Christ (Matthew 10:34)

Prologue

Timothy McVeigh, Meet Wayne Snell

Mountain Home, Arkansas

In the dawn of 1984, I stood on the frozen shores of Bull Shoals Lake in northern Arkansas searching for the place. *Zarepath Horeb*, the survivalist community called itself, a name taken from a Biblical site where ritual purification took place. Locals, however, referred to the commune as the "Jonestown of the Ozarks." With good reason as it turned out. In 1984, I was a reporter sent to cover the outbreak of far-right violence that was seemingly flaring up all over the country.

It had begun a year earlier when a 63-year-old North Dakota grandfather named Gordon Kahl slaughtered two federal marshals and wounded three others who'd tried to arrest him on a minor tax violation. Kahl, a member of a shadowy antigovernment organization called the Posse Comitatus, somehow eluded a massive manhunt for six months. On June 3, 1983, he was cornered a few miles from where I now stood. Kahl murdered again: this time a popular Arkansas sheriff, Gene Matthews, who had tried to talk him into surrendering. Kahl was incinerated in the onslaught that followed. Oddly, the farmhouse, actually a fortified bunker, where Kahl took refuge belonged to 61-year-old Leonard Ginter and his 58-year-old wife, Norma. They considered the murderer a hero.

In the months ahead, the nation would be rocked by a series of bloody and sensational crimes linked to an array of extremist groups. In the South, the Ku Klux Klan was calling for armed revolution, its members swapping their sheets for camouflage fatigues. Farmers, suffering the worst crisis since the Depression, were shouting about conspiracies involving Zionists and international bankers. Some were picking up guns to defend their homesteads. In Idaho, members of a neo-Nazi cell led by Robert Matthews were planning the assassination of liberal Denver talk-radio host Alan Berg, a crime they committed, then followed with a spree of terror bombings, shootings and robberies intended to trigger a fascist revolution.

Like the pristine forests of the Pacific Northwest, the somnolent green belt stretching across northern Arkansas and southern Missouri had become home to hundreds of extremists: survivalists, religious fanatics worshipping an Aryan Christ, white supremacists, neo-Nazis, Klansmen and nascent "patriot" militias. One of the most bizarre and violent of these groups, *Zarepath Horeb*, better known as The Covenant, the Sword, the Arm of the Lord (CSA), had brought me to the lakeshore.

"That's it," Gene Irby said, pointing to a cluster of buildings barely visible across the shore front.

"Where?" I said, straining to see through the swirling, windblown snow.

Irby was an Arkansas state trooper, one of the few outsiders the CSA communards deigned to acknowledge. In Little Rock, his boss, Colonel Tommy Goodwin, had arranged for me to ride with Irby to Bull Shoals Lake, an assignment that didn't exactly thrill the officer. I was hoping he could get me inside the camp. Irby took a deep breath, started the car and we were off.

Snow covered the rutted roads, frozen streams cracked and groaned as we crisscrossed the lake's tangled shores. Inlets and promontories, veined by unmarked, dead-end roads, slowed us to a crawl. January's pale light was fast disappearing, and, with it, any hope of reaching the place before dark. Not a soul stirred; no sound echoed on the great lake but the shuffing tires of Irby's police cruiser and the faint crackle of its radio.

Finally, on a crudely lettered sign hung from a barbed wire fence, the words *Zarepath Horeb* appeared. For eight years more than 200 men, women and children had gathered inside, girding themselves for the race war they believed would signal the "End Time" of American society. An Armageddon they described in loving detail in the CSA *Journal*:

> Parents will eat their children. . . . Communists will kill white Christians and mutilate them. Witches and Satanic Jews will offer people to their Gods. . . . Blacks will rape and kill white women. Homosexuals will sodomize whoever they can. . . .

Their leader was a bearded, pot-bellied preacher from San Antonio named James Ellison who'd arrived in the Ozarks in

1976, determined, he wrote, "to separate ourselves from everything unclean." The same Ellison reportedly who stripped his disciples of personal property and assets, who took multiple wives citing the need to germinate his "white seed," who stockpiled automatic weapons, explosives and, true to his Jonestown image, a drum of cyanide.

Thirty yards behind the fence was a log gatehouse that suggested a Hollywood version of a frontier stockade. A log was lowered across the dirt road like the arm of a highway toll booth. Nearby, I knew, was "Silhouette City," a target range where Ellison's fatigue-clad disciples fired at images of Golda Meir and Menachem Begin. Faint light glimmered from a number of ramshackle buildings I could see in the distance.

We sat there in darkness. Irby flashed his headlights and began to rhythmically honk the car's horn. Nothing. The commune's phone service had long been disconnected, so no one had any prior notice of our arrival. Ten minutes passed. Then Irby, dressed in civilian clothes, swung open the driver's door and stepped outside.

He hesitated a moment, then pulled out a short-barreled revolver and placed it on the front seat.

"Use it," he said, "if you need it."

I stared at him and then at the gun. A moment later he disappeared through the gate. The gate, as it turned out, was the entrance to a bad dream, a lawless, no-man's-land that somehow existed a few hundred yards from vacation homes and fishing lodges in the heart of the United States of America.

Irby had been gone almost half an hour, when, through the snow dusting the windshield, I glimpsed men silhouetted against the trees. They moved behind me, blocking the road that led away from the gate.

I groaned.

I needed to get out and identify myself as a reporter, to hide behind my thin plastic badge. I reached for Irby's pistol, fumbled off the safety and jammed it into the pocket of my black parka, cracked open the door of the car and stepped outside. The men, bundled in ragged clothes and military surplus jackets, were pointing rifles at me. I held my hands away from my coat and moved slowly toward the nearest one.

He was short, stocky, in his fifties, with glasses and a full beard.

"I'm Vince Coppola, a reporter for *Newswe* . . ."

The man's eyes were dead, his pale face expressionless. I stared at him and he stared back. I sensed it was useless to talk to him. We might have been from different planets.

Five months later, I saw this man again in a newspaper photograph. His name was Richard Wayne Snell, and he'd murdered an Arkansas trooper named Louis Bryant. The officer, a black man, had stopped Snell on a routine traffic violation. Snell, a so-called Identity Christian who believed nonwhites were subhuman, shot Bryant 11 times. For that crime, Snell, like Gordon Kahl, would become a hero in what the far right was calling the Second American Revolution.

Cornered by police in Broken Bow, Oklahoma, Snell was shot seven times and somehow survived. A pistol found in his van tied Snell to the November 1983 murder of a pawnshop owner named William Stumpp. Snell, believing Stumpp to be a Jew, executed him in the course of a robbery. He would be sentenced to death for that crime.

Wayne Snell, who called himself one of God's "dragons," survived to spread his wings over the Alfred P. Murrah Federal Building in Oklahoma City eleven years later. He survived, a hero, in the twisted hearts and minds of accused bombers Timothy McVeigh and Terry Nichols. And, as the world is learning, in their deeds.

Snell had been a frequent visitor to another survivalist commune, Elohim City, on the Oklahoma-Arkansas border, a place I would later visit. There he was befriended by Robert Millar, Elohim City's founder and religious leader. In the ten years Snell spent on Death Row, Millar became his spiritual adviser. Millar promised Snell he would claim his body for burial at Elohim City after his execution.

In October 1993, Timothy McVeigh was pulled over for a traffic infraction on Route 220, the only road running into the isolated compound. Two weeks before the Oklahoma bombing, phone records show McVeigh made a call to Elohim City. To this day, Robert Millar denies knowing McVeigh and says he never visited the commune.

On April 19, the day of Snell's execution, a Ryder truck allegedly rented by McVeigh, containing a 5,000-pound ammonium nitrate and fuel oil bomb exploded outside the Alfred P. Murrah Federal Building in Oklahoma City, killing 169 men, women and children and injuring 500 others.

A fake driver's license McVeigh was carrying when he was arrested shortly after the bombing listed his birthday as April 19.

As Richard Wayne Snell was being led to his execution, he turned and spoke his last words, "Look over your shoulder, justice is coming."

There was more. FBI agents raided David Koresh's Branch Davidian compound in Waco, Texas, on April 19, 1993, a debacle that left 75 people dead, including 20 children, and galvanized antigovernment hatred and far-right militia activity across the country.

"Vince. . . ."

I spun around. Gene Irby had returned, accompanied by a stocky, bald man wearing glasses, grimy jeans, a sweater under an army fatigue jacket. This was Kerry Noble, one of CSA's elders, men who wore military berets and fancied themselves Old Testament patriarchs. Irby introduced us.

I held out my hand. Noble refused to shake it.

"I'd like to ask you guys a few questions," I tried. "Maybe clear up some misconceptions."

"I'd have to pray over that," Noble said, "before talking to a reporter."

"I'll come back later or tomorrow," I said.

"I'd have to get permission from Pastor Ellison."

"That's fine."

"He's not here."

"When will . . . ?"

"It's impossible." Noble snapped. "Another time."

"Come on, man."

I'd driven six hours to stand scared and freezing at this gate. I persisted, firing questions. I could sense Irby was about to interrupt me, but I had a story to file.

"Your damn phone is disconnected," I said. "How will you know I'm coming?"

Noble put his nose in my face. I could smell his breath.

"Why can't you leave us alone!" he roared. "Leave us alone!"

With the shout, the gunmen scrambled toward us. Irby, muttering an obscenity, took me by the elbow and walked me to the car. He opened the door and shoved me inside. He walked to the driver's side, jumped in, started the engine. He threw the vehicle into reverse and we skidded down the icy track. Trapped in our headlights, Noble and his ragged band flared and then diminished in the swirling darkness. Like Snell, they called themselves Dragons of God

That image stayed with me as I drove out of the mountains back to Little Rock. The Dragons stayed with me long after the magazine stories I'd been working on were complete. I wanted to know more, to understand these odd people, this alienation. Was the escalating right-wing violence the mirror image of the left-wing radicalism of the sixties? Had Ronald Reagan, as some were suggesting, not taken the country far enough rightward to satisfy those on the fringe?

I wanted to talk firsthand, not just to the handful of leaders and violent criminals suddenly in the news, but to the sympathizers and the uncertain. I also wanted to interview their neighbors, heartland Americans who struggled to hold onto farm or family but shouted "No!" to hatred and violence. I wanted to document the far right's grievances, observe the rhythms and routines of these lives. Discover what America they inhabited.

Over the next years, I journeyed again into the heart of this darkness. When they'd have me, I visited the communes and compounds, the white-washed churches and country porches, the prisons, where my Dragons dwelled. When they'd let me, I talked to their wives and children, the neighbors, the rural law-men and judges often drawn unwillingly into the web. Where I could, I traveled back in time, to the Depression and the great immigrant migrations at the turn of the century, trying to trace such virulence to its roots. Those journeys, separate yet con-nected, are the basis of this book.

The men and women I encountered imagined themselves besieged patriots, alienated and frustrated at every turn. America, they cried, had drifted far from the Founding Fathers' dream of a white, Christian nation. Jews and non-white "mud races" were defiling the Promised Land. Life had become bitter. The farms and factories were closing, small towns emptying, the fabric of society shredding. Crime went unpunished, school prayers unsaid; divorce, abortion, drug abuse, homosexuality threatened.

Immigrant hordes, who knew or cared nothing about George Washington, were pouring into the country. Honesty and hard work no longer guaranteed success. Millions of white Americans had not achieved affluence or middle-class status even after many generations. Their names—Miller and Smith, Butler and Black—ran back into history, filling out the tax rolls and military musters. What dark conspiracy held them back?

In the cities, people got rich manipulating paper while farmers were forced to sell their crops for less than it cost to coax them from the soil. The government, now called ZOG, for Zionist Occupation Government, was in the hands of "One-Worlders" who conspired to rule the earth. The media, part of the conspiracy, poured out a steady stream of filth and deception.

A handful of people believed only divine intervention could save the country; others prepped for violent revolution. They did not see themselves as terrorists. *Patriot* was the term they most often used. They espoused quintessential values, talked endlessly about God and country, prayed a lot, loved children. Their heroes were Thomas Jefferson and James Maddison. They studied the Scriptures and the Constitution, imagining simple answers to complex, perhaps insoluble problems: America would become the Promised Land, evil-doers would be punished, the lousy job and the cramped trailer would vanish, the bankrupt farm saved from auction on the courthouse steps. Children wouldn't use drugs or run off.

Somehow, genocide peacefully coexisted in their heads with Jesus, mom and apple pie.

I was there in the spring of 1985, when 300 federal and state officers sealed off the CSA compound on Bull Shoals Lake in Arkansas. Ellison, shielding himself by marching women and children in front of the lawmen's guns, surrendered after 72 hours. By then, two state policemen and a sheriff were dead in the Ozarks; a synagogue, a gay church and a natural gas pipeline had been bombed. I followed Ellison when he was convicted of federal racketeering and conspiracy charges and was sentenced to 20 years in prison. I saw him released, heard he too had disappeared into Elohim City.

In the 1990s, I watched the Dragons—the anti-Semites, racists, Identity Christians, neo-Nazis—quietly infect the emergent citizens militias like viruses. I saw the radicals win support from an increasingly angry and alienated segment of the population. The federal government—in the rebels' minds bloated, corrupt, anti-life, anti-gun, Constitutiondenying, conspiratorial—became a hated enemy, its citizens too often innocent targets. Federal agents killed or jailed dime-store Hitlers like CSA's James Ellison and The Order's Robert Matthews, only to face the amorphous "leaderless resistance" that led to the bombing in Oklahoma City.

In Idaho, on Ruby Ridge, the FBI agents who needlessly assaulted the cabin of Randy Weaver, a white supremacist wanted for selling two sawed-off shotguns, played right into the extremists' hands: they killed Weaver's 14-year-old son Samuel and his wife Vicki, 43, in August 1992. The murder of William Degan, a U.S. deputy marshal also killed in the attack, went unavenged when Idaho jurors acquitted Weaver and another radical named Kevin Harris.

"Baby killers! Baby killers!" Weaver's neighbors had screamed.

Around the country, thousands of militiamen were enraged. "Never again," they vowed.

In the flames of David Koresh's Branch Davidian compound, thousands of displaced and impassioned men saw a justification for the horror of Oklahoma City. Hatred was sown like dragons' teeth. In the piteous ruins of the Alfred P. Murrah Federal Building, Timothy McVeigh became Wayne Snell.

Christ was a bigot. I'm proud to be one.

Tom Corsaut, Identity Christian

Chapter 1

The Identity Christians

La Porte, Colorado

I'm sitting, waiting, on a sofa in the living room of Pastor Pete Peters' ranch house in La Porte, north of Denver. Around me, half a dozen middle-aged women dressed in pants suits the color of Easter eggs chatter about children, recipes, the cost of living. I relax, let myself drift in the familiar, comforting drone of conversation. Ten minutes drift by, then the pastor's attractive wife, Cheri, turns to me.

"You look like a Jew," she says with a smile.

"Excuse me?"

"You a Jew?"

The other women perk up, coffee cups tinkling in their saucers.

"No," I answer. "I went to Catholic school for 12 years. You know, Catholic like the Pope."

"But you *look* like a Jew."

"What do you mean? . . . Like with horns? I'm Italian. Italian. My uncle is Sonny Giordano. . . ."

"No . . . silly," Mrs. Peters titters and turns back to her friends, who feign embarrassment.

I shrug, excuse myself. My ex-wife is Jewish and I guess my daughter is, too. I'd like to smack this woman in the pastel pants suit.

On August 28, 1992, Cheri's husband, Pete Peters, a longtime Identity preacher, had sent a letter to Randy Weaver, then barricaded in his cabin on Ruby Ridge urging him to surrender. Three days later, Weaver walked off the mountain and the siege ended. Peters, no slouch when it came to winning publicity for himself and his movement, spent the next four years using the Weaver and Branch Davidian tragedies as a spark to rally thousands of "patriots" to confront the "injustice and tyranny" of the government killings.

Outside, a misty rain is falling. Peters and a dozen men, all members of his Identity Christian congregation, are struggling to erect a patched army tent for a children's Bible camp he's hosting.

That morning I'd attended services at Peters' church, bright with whitewashed walls and stained glass. Fifty people filled the pews, neatly dressed, well-groomed young marrieds with toddlers, teenagers, single women, grandmas and grandpas in their seventies. Their hymns—"The Old Rugged Cross" and "Lily of the Valley"—floated out to a meadow where sheep, bells tinkling, grazed peacefully.

The deacon hesitates as I ask to take Communion, then passes the tray of shot glasses filled with grape juice and tiny, rectangular wafers my way. During the service, an older woman named Azelie Fleitas smiles, takes my hand, then whispers an invitation to a potluck dinner. Later she will pile my plate with fried chicken, potato salad and sugary home-made cookies.

Dressed in a white sport jacket, girdled by a belt with a big silver buckle, Peters harangues his congregation with a sermon that, among other things, identifies Washington, D.C., and Manhattan as vast Satanic playgrounds where biblical allegories have sprung to life.

The "Abomination of Desolation," an idol erected by the Syrian king Antiochus, Peters announces, —I'm sitting there blinking— is standing in Rockefeller Center. The Washington Monument is really a pagan statue erected by Nebuchadnezzar (Daniel 3:1-8). Another biblical idol, Peter says, mentioned in Daniel 2:31-35 as being made of gold, silver, brass, iron and clay, represents race-mixing. There's more: its toes are the ten regions of the Federal Emergency Management Administration (FEMA), a bureaucracy set up to establish concentration camps across the United States.

"Ooohs" and "aahhs" escape the congregation.

"Imagine an eight-year-old blonde girl being bused into Harlem!" Peters thunders shifting into the here and now. The Caucasian race, he laments, is being out-propagated by blacks and illegal aliens "who suck out our nation's sustenance!"

"Amen!" come the shouts from the back of the church.

Peters is just warming up, a white-bread preacher striving for the rhythms and routines, the stutters and ululations, of black ministers in Georgia, Alabama, and elsewhere in the South. Farmers, he chants, are "cry babies squealing like gut-shot panthers." Not crying out to God but to "Uncle Sugar Teat who's been stabbing them in the back for 40 years!"

The Judeo-Christian God is a "giant marshmallow floating

in the sky . . . Mmmm . . . my God is angry!"

Other preachers? Pimps and prostitutes, Peters shouts, shamelessly promoting Jews as the Chosen People. "They know who butters their bread and who owns the media!" he shouts. "And they have the audacity to accuse me of trying to overthrow the U.S. government? I just want it back!"

"Amen! . . . Amen! Say on!" come the shouts. A woman stands arms upraised. Sweating, Peters walks from the altar.

Among Identity Christians, meekness is no virtue. Turning the other cheek is pure cowardice. In this religion, blacks and minorities are "pre-Adamic" mud races. Over the last decade, far-right groups like The Order, Posse Comitatus, Ku Klux Klan, skinheads, and an increasing number of militias have woven Identity "truths" into their nightmare scenarios for America. Racial identity is the thread that ties disparate crazies together, that turns isolated hatemongers into crusading zealots.

"Identity breaks the power Jewry has over America," Arkansas Klansman Thom Robb tells me. "And the fear driven into people's hearts by Jerry Falwell and other so-called preachers: 'If you don't bless the Jews God will curse you.'"

"Now, we're Israel! We don't have to play pansy with the Jews anymore."

Identity has two premises: Jesus Christ was an Aryan, and the people of Britain and northern Europe are the ten Lost Tribes of Israel. It follows then that they are the Chosen People. The Bible is their book. America is the new Israel, the Promised Land.

British-Israelism, as the sect is known in the United Kingdom, has been around for hundreds of years. Its prophet may have been Richard Brothers, an 18th-century Englishman who declared himself "Prince of the Hebrews." Brothers theorized that the British were descendants of Israelites carried into ancient Media (northwestern Iran), where, over time, they evolved into the Sacae or Scythians. This horde eventually moved over the Caucasus Mountains into northern Europe. The Sacae became the Saxons.

According to Brothers and his disciples, the Bible prophesied Israel would change its name and be located on "the isles." The word "British," they decided, was derived from the Hebrew *Berit-ish*, meaning "man of the covenant."

No one could prove the Sacae became Saxons or that the Sacae were Israelites. In ancient Hebrew, for example, references to *isle* or *isles* could apply to any coast that was separated from Palestine by water. Therefore *Israel* could include Greece, Italy, Egypt and most of Asia Minor, as well as England. Could a language be forgotten so completely by its people? Peculiar Hebrew customs—circumcision, a woman's uncleanness, for example—have no Anglo-Saxon counterparts. Not a problem, says Pete Peters. "It was God's *intention* that our Identity be lost. It's the price of sinfulness.

"Our very ignorance is proof we are right."

In the 19th century, a book written by Edward Hind—*Identification of the British Nations with Lost Israel*—sold an astounding 250,000 copies. At the time, Anglo-Israelism was not anti-Semitic. Nor was it exclusionary. Christ kept his Jewish roots. The Jews were two tribes, Judah and Levi, that would eventually be reunited with the other ten. In fact, in 1947, British-Israelists, by then a minuscule cult, hailed the establishment of the nation of Israel.

In the United States after World War II, a renegade Methodist minister named Wesley Swift added his own hate-filled ravings to the sect. "All Jews must be destroyed," Swift wrote. "I prophecy . . . there will not be a Jew in the United States, and by that I mean a Jew who will be able to walk or talk." From the fevered brain of Bertrand L. Comparet, an attorney who followed Swift's teaching, came the "Two Seed Theory," the notion that Adam and Eve produced Abel and the white race; the Serpent bedded Eve, producing Cain . . . and the Jews.

The Identity message affects people in Peters' congregation differently. Nancy Fleitas, a court reporter, says she experiences "a feeling of purpose and responsibility." She and her parents, Art and Azelie, drifted through Methodist, Seventh Day Adventist and Church of Christ congregations before finding Peters. Sweet-faced and overweight, Nancy skis, plays tennis and rides her bike. She reads John Grisham novels and self-help books. She'd like to find a husband, but the men she meets are not up to her standards or are not interested.

In Denver, friends think her religion is "off the wall." But Nancy, her life circumscribed by loneliness and need, knows better. "I'm a member of a Chosen People," she tells me. "I have an obligation to teach by example. To do what my race is supposed to do according to God's plan."

At the potluck dinner, a blond, bearded man stares as Nancy and I talk. He walks closer, then drifts back against a wall. He does this a few times, trying to catch snatches of our conversation. As she drifts off, he approaches. His name is Mike Longmore and he says he's an ex-marine. He wants to tell me his story.

"Sure, go ahead."

"I enlisted," he says as he wolfs down a plate piled high with ham and potato salad, "because I was intent on destroying anything I could, especially if it was human. I wanted to go wherever they'd pay me to kill.

"And I wanted to come home dead."

Longmore, short and wiry as a speed freak, is an encyclopedia of racial grief. Unemployed for eight months, he's supporting himself doing odd jobs. Seething as he watches well-dressed professionals zip by in their BMWs and Porches. An outsider, staring at his reflection in the windows of Denver's crowded restaurants and bars. Once he starts talking, bitterness tumbles out of him like a poisoned stream. "I was white and it was my fault that blacks were discriminated against. . . . My teachers taught me it was my duty to commit suicide.

"I decided to take as many with me as I could."

After high school, he joined the military. Discipline was hard for him to take, especially when it was enforced by black sergeants who towered over him, who ragged him, daring him to stand up to them, to act on his feelings.

With no wars raging, Longmore says he banked his homicidal impulses with drink and pills. In an alley, he says, he discovered "Satan is as real as the person sitting next to you." Discharged, he drifted, stumbling from one town, one gig, one humiliation to another. When he arrived in La Porte, Peters was leading what had been a traditional Church of Christ congregation into the brave new world of Identity Christianity.

Many fled the church.

But Longmore was intoxicated with the new theology. Conspiratorial Christianity served him well. Now he understood why he was always the outsider. Enemies were plotting against him, stacking the odds against his success. God, through Pete Peters' ministry, opened his eyes. Identity has given him a purpose. He will be one of God's Dragons. A Kamakazi waiting for the divine wind.

"Christ said 'Love your enemies,'" Longmore says, his face a few inches from mine. "He didn't say 'Love my enemies.' We want biblical law enacted. We are unforgiving. That's what makes us so violent. People must pay a physical price for physical sins. A murderer dies for his sin." He looks hard at me, then adds, "I hold abortion to be murder."

A girl, no more than a teenager, walks by. Eager to fulfill Peters' command that Aryans multiply, Longmore darts after her. "What I want most," he says, "is a good woman by my side."

Tom Corsaut nods his head vigorously. Nearly 60, Corsaut moved to Colorado after his second marriage failed. He says he was drawn to Pete Peters' ministry like iron to a magnet. Unemployed, he's been sleeping in the church basement. He cites his pedigrees: John Birch Society, the American Nazi Party. "George Lincoln Rockwell (the assassinated Nazi leader) was right," says Corsaut, "but he didn't have a Christian perspective."

Corsaut is a type I will encounter again and again on the fringe, a being whose very existence is defined and informed by hatred—in Corsaut's case, deep-seated, virulent anti-Semitism. "Aryans . . . Identity . . . patriot militias." Corsaut mouths the right buzz words, but what he is really all about is hating Jews. "Eighty-five percent of modern Jewry cannot trace themselves to Abraham," he tells me. "They are the synagogue of Satan."

His blue eyes flash.

"There's a battle for the planet," he says. "Between us and the people who hate Jesus Christ, who spit every time they mention his name. The Jews!"

Israel will be destroyed, he tells me, "by a humongous tragedy." The *intifada* battles then raging in the West Bank and Gaza, the Hizbollah guerrillas firing Katusha rockets from Southern Lebanon, are joys to Corsaut.

"Our enemies are trying to smear us. They call us bigots and racists. A bigot is a person who believes in one way of doing things. *Christ was a bigot!* I'm proud to be one."

Pastor Peters watches, tugging his mustache, as Corsaut, Longmore, and a man named Fred Blodgett, who restores Packard automobiles, tear away the veil of fellowship I'd felt inside the church. When Blodgett tells me that Denver talk-radio host Alan Berg (killed by neo-Nazis) was *really* murdered by his employers because of failing ratings, Peters pulls me aside. These men, he whispers, do not necessarily reflect the philosophy of his church.

Of course he never mentions that two of Berg's killers, Robert Matthews and David Lane, visited his church. Zillah Craig, Matthews' mistress, was a member of the congregation. Another militant, an old man from Mississippi named Jack

Mohr who describes himself as a "brigadier general" in the Christian Patriots Defense League, has been showing up in La Porte to lecture on guerrilla warfare.

"There was a whole lot of hatred and animosity there," Peters says, attempting to put some distance between him and Berg's killers. Across the room is a catalog of his sermons available on audiotape. Among the titles, *Music to Kill By*.

Later, relaxing in his living room with Cheri cuddled next to him, Peters goes out of his way to make me, a visitor, comfortable. He holds a job with the Farmers Home Administration, he says. His hobby is busting broncos. He runs a Bible camp for kids in the summer. Peters gives me a kinder, gentler justification of Identity Christianity.

There's no doubt, he says, that the biblical Israelites are the forefathers of today's Anglo-Saxons. "In Genesis, God promised Abraham his seed would form a multitude of nations. The Jews have never formed a multitude. Of course we have." The fact that 90 percent of all missionaries come from England, America and Germany "proves that whites are chosen as God's servant race."

Playing the scholar, Peters cites historical precedents. "A hundred years ago, many people thought of America as the Promised Land. In old books, George Washington is referred to as the 'Leader of Israel.' When the Spanish Armada was sailing, Sir Francis Drake wrote a letter that said, 'Pray for Israel.'"

A church member named Mike Green, Bible in hand, jumps into the conversation. "Encyclopedias have been rewritten," he says. "Definitions changed. I read a new history book that said Paul Revere didn't make that ride. He was in bed with a whore!"

"What book was that?" I ask. "I'd like to see it."

"I'll find it for you," Green promises. "I'll mail it to you." He never does.

Peters, still uneasy about Corsaut and Longmore, wants to

talk about Jews. "They're not the cause of our problem," he shrugs. "Once we get our act cleaned up, *we'll* be blessed with peace and prosperity. Vince, let me tell you a story:

"A Jewish stockbroker comes up to me in Virginia. I had just preached a message on usury.

"He spoke the words 'How odd of God to choose . . .'"

"The Jews," I answer.

"Right! 'Pastor,' the stockbroker said, 'somebody has to charge interest. You must understand it doesn't make us happy.'

"This man had tremendous insight!" Peters exclaims.

Cheri nods approvingly. "He understood! *Somebody had to charge it!* How could I condemn him? It's God's judgment, God's design!"

That's it! I thought. Jews, like Milton's Lucifer, are part of God's plan. A notion lost on the cab drivers, dry cleaners and candy-store owners I knew struggling to make a living in Brooklyn. It strikes me that Peters and his flock exist, not so much in a different place from the rest of us, but in a different dimension, divided by a membrane through which reason, love, compassion and understanding cannot pass.

Concepts of destiny and free will are swirling around the coffee table. Charity and anti-Semitism war in Peters' heart.

"Your family came from Italy, right?" he asks.

"Yeah." (Here we go, I'm thinking.)

"You do know that the biggest share of the Mafia are Jewish. They were expelled from Italy to Sicily."

"No, I didn't know that. That's pretty interesting, in fact. I grew up in a neighborhood with a lot of Mafia guys . . ."

"See." He smiles, happy to help me.

I ask about the future. "Oh, there will probably be war," he says, sipping his coffee. "Christians are not pacifists. The Pilgrims were God-fearing, but they shot Indians. George Washington wasn't a pacifist. The conflict will be started by conspiratorial forces manipulating immigrants from

Indochina and Central America. When the dust settles, tri-umphant white separatists will strictly enforce God's law.

"There are no provisions for prison in the Bible. Murderers, kidnappers, would be executed, along with practicing homo-sexuals."

Only God will determine the time frame. Peters says he's unhappy that "hate groups have taken Identity trappings and march under our banner. They use these truths to bolster their egos, and as a justification to go out and hang Jews. Frankly, they are puffed up and arrogant. Our perspective breeds humility, because we never have been faithful to God.

"As for believing that Jews are . . . uh . . . the result of Satan's cohabitation with Eve . . . " Peters pauses, then adds, "we reject that. We don't think Satan has a penis."

I left La Porte, driving north to Laramie, then west on Interstate 80 across the lonely, boulder-strewn hills of Wyoming. Instead of cattle, there were flocks of sheep; instead of spring sunshine, snow showers. Many hours later, I arrived in Cokeville, a depressed mining town (population 550) in Wyoming's extreme southwest corner. I parked my car and walked down Main Street eager for a drink, a snack, a conversation. Many of the stores were shuttered, those still in business, poorly stocked.

Children, riding their bikes, glanced at me fearfully, then darted away. Others froze midstep in sidewalk games as my shadow passed over them. A month before, an extremist named David Young and his wife had walked into Cokeville's elementary school with a powerful bomb and many guns. They took 160 children—the town's only treasure—hostage, and demanded $300 million and a direct line to the White House. Young called this assault "the Biggie."

Two hours later the bomb went off. A teacher was shot, dozens of students badly hurt in the ensuing chaos.

The sunlit fears of the kids were Young's work. In him, the

secret dread of every American law enforcement agent had come to pass: a terrorist had targeted a community and he'd been unstoppable. Young had *worked* as a policeman in Cokeville. He was tough, aggressive, very much like Richard Jewell, the gung-ho security officer who earlier this year had been suspected of planting a bomb in Atlanta's Centennial Olympic Park.

In Cokeville, Young the policeman wore a flat-brimmed Stetson and carried two pearl-handled Colt revolvers on his gunbelt. He saw himself as Wyatt Earp; on Main Street, the giggling kids called him "Dudley Do-Right" after the bumbling cartoon figure.

"He'd stand there at the old Stockman Hotel spinning those guns," Cokeville mayor John Dayton tells me. "He didn't spin them for long. I fired him." Young, a creature of vaunting ego, wrote *philosopher* on an application for his next job, a heavy equipment operator. He spent seven years in the choking heat and dust of the phosphate mines, a man who, in his own mind, walked with Socrates. And planned his revenge.

"I'm down on everything in this culture," Young scrawled in a thousand-page diary he used to catalog his intellectual meanderings, his gas mileage, bowel movements, the times he had sex, with whom and how. Among the pages was a plastic bag containing a used condom, labeled "Margaret 1963."

He'd flirted with the Posse Comitatus, a violent far-right organization that recognized no authority above the county, but even that group was too much control for him to stomach. Young, like so many on the fringe, believed he could personally fire a national revival. "David had his own ideas on how the world should work," his stepdaughter Bernie Peterson says. "Only he could run the government."

Like other extremists, he couldn't let go of the society he scorned. If his brilliance was not appreciated in this world, Young decided he would move on to the next. Death was a portal; he'd carry the children far from the corrupt influences of society. He was a Pied Piper, a patriot; his name would live on in history. He ordered his wife, Dorsie, to bring her make-up kit on the trip to the "brave new world" he imagined awaited him.

In the classroom, Young waited for his impossible ransom surrounded by trembling children. "He had no intention of coming out of there alive as we know alive," says Ron Hartley, the Lincoln County investigator who discovered Young's diary. Four of Hartley's kids were hostages in that classroom.

The bomb went off prematurely when Dorsie inadvertently tripped a "dead man's switch," a clothespin that kept the device's electrical contacts apart. Furious, Young blew his wife's brains out with a .44 caliber revolver, then walked into a tiny bathroom and shot himself as children and teachers scrambled to escape the smoke and flame. When it was over, Hartley discovered two of the bomb's blasting caps intact. Leaking gasoline had soaked other components preventing the device from exploding properly. "It didn't explode, it ignited," he says. "Had it exploded, it would have taken the walls down."

I spent two days in this grim place, talking to children terrified of the *stranger* who came in the night to poison their dreams. But Cokeville would rally; it was a community determined to exorcise the demons Young had unleashed. Days after the blast, psychologist Nohl Sandall led the victims back into the ruined classroom. Smoke had discolored the walls, Dorsie's blood stained the carpeting, but here and there was a book bag or lunch box a child could reclaim. "They came out in a state of panic," Sandall tells me. "It was important to go back in and reestablish ownership, to replace the horror."

As I talked to the younger children, I noticed that an awful new word had entered their vocabularies: *terrorize*. Cokeville, scorched by dragon fire, was rallying. Oklahoma City and other horrors were looming.

Today it finally began. After all these years of talking . . . . We are at war with the System and it is no longer a war of words.

— *The Turner Diaries*

Chapter 2

The Aryans of Idaho

Coeur D'Alene

There is a freshness in the air, a mountain tang of pine and new-cut hay. The streams, crystal clear and cold, feed pristine lakes that mirror the surrounding forests. The traveler coming out of the East into northern Idaho takes an odd, possessive pride in this beauty: America in its purple-mountained majesty.

I drive quickly past the dying towns of Kellogg and Wallace, where unemployment in the mines tops 50 percent, and into Coeur D'Alene, a 1950s vintage resort detailed down to the malt shops and pre-fast food hamburger joints. Like most of Idaho, Coeur D'Alene is populated by white people. Of the state's roughly one million residents, 96 percent are white. For two decades, white supremacists have been trickling in, seeing in Idaho's pale faces and open spaces an invitation to the Promised Land.

In 1973, a retired aeronautical engineer named Richard Girnt Butler crossed into Idaho, where he set up his Church of Jesus Christ Christian and its infamous Aryan Nations political arm in tiny Hayden Lake. No one realized it, but Butler guaranteed that Coeur D'Alene would be known across America as a place to fear and avoid.

He was joined by his "kinsman" Keith Gilbert, pastor of the Restored Church of Jesus Christ, an institution that venerated Hitler as the reincarnation of the prophet Elijah. According to Gilbert, "Elijah" published a work that made the Scriptures accessible to 20th-century man: *Mein Kampf.*

In 1966, Gilbert attempted to detonate 1,400 pounds of dynamite at a Los Angeles B'nai B'rith meeting where Martin Luther King, Jr., was the featured speaker. He spent five years in San Quentin for his trouble. Upon his release, he showed up in Idaho, determined to fulfill his ministry. He liked to be photographed posing in a stiff-armed Nazi salute alongside a "Welcome to Idaho" sign. In 1982, Gilbert began stalking Connie Fort, a single parent with children of mixed race. He called her eight-year-old son a "nigger," then began playing "chicken" with them if they crossed the street. When Fort protested, Coeur D'Alene police reportedly told her to make "a citizen's arrest."

When I arrive in Coeur D'Alene in the mid-1980s, Gilbert is in jail for welfare fraud.

Others followed Gilbert's hateful lead. A Hispanic family was ordered out of Coeur D'Alene. When they didn't move quickly enough, their house was set afire. Next, the family dog's throat was slashed. A caller promised the same for the children. In Post Falls, a Korean child was spat upon in a restaurant, an adoption agency trying to place minority children was threatened. In Hayden Lake, restaurant owner Sid Rosen found his establishment decorated with swastikas and the words "Jew swine." Rosen sold the business.

There was something else, a complacency, perhaps, that allowed the extremists to take hold. A mood, a state of mind, maybe naiveté, but it was there. The great majority of Idahoans had never been pressed. Along with its sister states— Wyoming, Montana, Oregon and Washington—Idaho had never been touched by the civil rights and other liberation movements. Stereotypes remained frozen and unchallenged. Whites fleeing California tended to support the xenophobia of the locals.

Politicians were slow to respond to the hatemongers, who grew ever bolder. When Coeur D'Alene's Chamber of Commerce finally got around to denouncing the blatant acts of racial harassment taking place, its statement began, "To promote and protect a positive business climate."

Not much had changed. One weekend night I sat in a Coeur D'Alene hotel listening to a French Canadian singer named Carol Stirn. Dark-haired and lovely, Stirn played many of the small clubs in northern Idaho. As she performed with her band, I watched men walk up to her handing her pieces of paper.

"Requests for songs," I thought.

Later, as I sat drinking beer with Stirn and her husband, Mike, she unfolded one of the slips of paper.

"Get off the stage you fucking Jew!" it read.

A Malicious Harassment law was passed in Idaho in the 1980s, but by then the extremists were so entrenched that Butler, Gilbert and a virulent Klansman named Louis Beam attended public hearings and denounced the harassment law as an assault on their freedom of speech.

By then a much more serious threat was growing. Robert Jay Matthews, one of Richard Butler's violence-prone disciples, broke from Aryan Nations and founded The Order. Unlike Butler, Matthews and his band of neo-Nazis did not plan to harass their enemies. They would kill them. Matthews declared war on America. Unwilling, Coeur D'Alene, Idaho, would be his capital city.

> *Rise, from your graves white brothers. The Aryan yeomanry is awakening. A long forgotten wind is starting to blow. Do you hear approaching thunder? War is upon the land. The tyrant's blood will flow.*
>
> —The Order's Declaration of War

They came for Alan Berg the way they'd always come for Jews. On the night of June 18, 1984, four men lay in wait near his townhouse at 1445 Adams Street in Denver. Berg, one of talk radio's pioneers, was returning from a dinner date with his ex-wife.

As always, he was manic and hyper, his thoughts bouncing between Chicago, where Berg, a lawyer and recovering alcoholic, had had more than his share of bad times, and Denver, where he had a new, young girlfriend, a skyrocketing career. Should he remarry? Reconcile with Judith? Move to a bigger market? Decisions and choices, a thousand things pulling him in different directions. Berg lit a Pall Mall as he pulled his black VW convertible into his driveway; he grabbed the bag of dog food he had picked up for Fred, his airedale.

He was halfway out of the car when a man emerged from the shadows. The man was tall and muscular with an odd, sloping nose. Berg's eyes darted to the silencer-equipped machine gun cradled in the man's arms and then up to the leering grin on his face.

"What?" Robbery? Revenge? Some stupid fucking half-assed joke? A thousand half-formed images flashed through Berg's careening mind as the killer raised the weapon. To him, Alan Berg was not a man. He was a Jew, less than a dog. The gun chattered, a 13-round burst that hit Berg 12 times, then jammed. The impact of the bullets jerked Berg sideways like a marionette, mashing his face and skull like a ripe cantaloupe.

The killer, Bruce Carroll Pierce, was, like his leader, Robert Jay Matthews, a member of The Order, a.k.a. Bruders Schweigen (Silent Brotherhood), neo-Nazis who had plunged far beyond the ranting of the fanatic right. They saw themselves as Aryan Crusaders who had declared war on the Zionist Occupation Government, the same ZOG that haunts the imagination of today's Freemen and patriot militias.

Alan Berg was their first victim. In 1996, he'd be rich, celebrated—Howard Stern with a crusading side. Twelve years ago, the tall, bearded, rail-thin jock outraged many of his rural listeners with combative, insult-driven rap. Berg was intense, insecure, but his show was always among KOA's most popular. His gravelly voice carried to places far beyond Denver's metropolitan area, places where irony and insult fed the flames of anti-Semitism and race hatred.

Berg enjoyed jerking the chains of the crazies who bombarded the station with biblical rant and threatening phone calls. A few years back, a burly Ku Klux Klansman named Fred Wilkins showed up at Berg's radio station, threatening to blow Berg away. Berg was also involved in a nasty libel lawsuit with Roderick Eliot, publisher of the *Primrose and Cattleman's Gazette*, an agricultural newsletter that seemed more interested in government conspiracies than crops or cattle. Another member of The Order's hit squad was David Lane, a Klansman who'd worked for Eliot. Lane, who drove the getaway car, was not the Aryan warrior he imagined himself; he shit in his pants as Pierce slaughtered Berg.

Robert Matthews was a short, stocky, 31-year-old who worked a small farm near Metaline Falls, Washington. He was married, had an adopted son and another child with his mistress, Zillah Craig. Matthews, who saw himself as a quintessential small-town American, volunteered as a wrestling coach at the local high school. A pleasant man, the other coaches thought, except for some "extremely strong convictions" about racial superiority. Matthews' farm was a few hours' drive from Hayden Lake, Idaho, where Butler had created Aryan Nations.

Matthews had been involved in tax protest and other right-wing causes since he was teenager. In Idaho, it was natural for him to be drawn to Aryan Nations' religious services, rallies and family gatherings. Under the tutelage of Richard Butler, he embraced Identity Christianity, the belief that Jesus was blue-eyed and fair of skin. Jews, descendants of a Mongolian tribe, the Khazars, were enemies. And Alan Berg was a Jew.

In the stillness of the Northwest, Matthews brooded over the tortured prose of turn-of-the-century "nativist" writers like Madison Grant (*The Passing of the Great Race*) and Theodore Lothrop Stoddard (*The Menace of the Under Man*). "I am a leader," he told himself. And the wind blowing through the pines whispered, "Destined for greatness."

For Matthews, writing was slow and painful, but he persisted, developing a style seemingly lifted from Norse sagas and fantasy comics. A style portentous enough to convey the malaise of a great race being brought to its knees: "My knowledge of ancient European subjects started to awaken a wrongfully suppressed emotion buried deep within my soul of racial pride and consciousness," he wrote. "The stronger my love for my people grew, the deeper became my hatred for those who would destroy my race, my heritage, darken the future of my children."

At the Aryan Nations compound, Matthews met the druggies and dishwashers, the loners and losers who would be captains in his army. Each man with a chip on his shoulder, a grudge or a grievance to justify his failure: Gary Lee

Yarbrough, a dishwasher who liked to stand alongside Richard Butler wearing a storm trooper's uniform; slender, ascetic David Tate, a dairy farmer's son commanded by God to carry a gun; Berg's killer, Bruce Carroll Pierce, a former *Atlanta Journal-Constitution* newspaper boy. David Lane, an impoverished drifter who haunted McDonald's restaurants, gorging himself on fast food and Matthews' overripe poems:

> *Give your soul to God and pick up your gun*
> *Time to deal in lead.*
> *We are the legions of the damned.*
> *The army of the already dead.*

That poem echoed the themes of one of Matthews' favorite books, the *Turner Diaries*, a clumsy, fascist thriller written by William Pierce, a Georgia-born physics professor who runs a neo-Nazi organization based in Washington, D.C., The National Alliance.

The book, which has now been studied and analyzed as thoroughly as *Beowulf*, depicts a bleeding America in the thrall of Zionists and their brutal minions. A great white hope appears, Earl Turner, a man in whom Matthews sees his own reflection. Turner wages guerrilla war against ZOG; an orgy of assassinations and bombings follow. Nuclear weapons are seized; the Soviet Union, Israel and the Pentagon are vaporized. Turner's execution squads purge the land of Jews, blacks and other undesirables.

Turner dies, but not before glimpsing victory.

It was all there, a blueprint for revolution, detailed right down to counterfeiting, terrorism, assassination. In September 1983, nine men gathered at Matthews' farm. They stood in a circle around a baby girl. "For blood, soil and honor, for the future of our children and our king, Jesus Christ," they pledged, "we commit ourselves to battle." And The Order was born.

Bizarre? Absurd? Insane? Perhaps, but in that ceremony lay the seed of the kind of insanity that would blossom in Oklahoma City 12 years later. In the 1990s Timothy McVeigh viewed *The Turner Diaries* as his bible, hawking it at gun fairs and militia gatherings. Fifteen others would eventually join Matthews' crusade, representing the fringe in all its lunatic colors: Identity Christians, Klansmen, Nazis, survivalists, fascist communards from Arkansas. A larger network of sympathizers and fellow travelers was in place around the country.

Matthews began his war by using the Aryan Nations printing press to churn out $500,000 in poor-quality counterfeit money. He wrote "An Open Letter to the U.S. Congress" taking lawmakers to task for Vietnam, street crime, affirmative action, illegal immigration, busing, the farm crisis and the oil embargo. He wrote law enforcement, the military, judges, legislators, bankers and businessmen, warning them that it was death to oppose him. He would hunt them down like dogs and "have their heads removed from their bodies." He told his men he would award them "points" for killing FBI agents.

By December, Matthews felt the exhilaration Earl Turner recorded in the first lines of the *Diaries*: "Today it finally began. After all these years of talking. . . . We are at war with the System, and it is no longer a war of words."

The war began with a whimper. On December 3, 1983, Bruce Carroll Pierce walked into a Yakima, Washington, shopping mall and passed a phony $50 bill. He was promptly arrested. On his person police found a leaflet for a racist convention that promised free admission to anyone who "brought his own little black boy for target practice." Pierce pleaded guilty to the counterfeiting charge and was sentenced to two years in prison. Given two weeks to set his affairs in order, he disappeared.

Matthews was more successful. On December 20, 1983, he and his accomplices robbed the City Bank of Innis Arden, Washington, of $26,000. In January, he took $3,600 from the

Washington Mutual Savings Bank in Spokane. In Seattle, an armored car was hit for $43,000, then another for $500,000. Automatic weapons, dynamite, hand grenades smuggled off military bases, nitroglycerine, were stockpiled. Matthews bought police scanners, CB radios, computers; even a "voice stress analyzer" to test the loyalty of his men.

And always the clouds of fantasy covered Matthews' eyes. He budgeted $100,000 for Project Reliance, a scheme developed by a local chemist that was supposed to use hair from a man's head to control his mind.

He bought land near Priest River, Idaho, and set up the "Timberline Hunting Club," a Nazi boot camp complete with its own cook. Safe houses were established in Boise and on Whidbey Island, 50 miles from Seattle. A "National Command" sent out military-style orders to his soldiers on how to equip and conduct themselves.

While Matthews played Aryan general, his dysfunctional troops bragged, fought, spent money on stereos, chased women and got stoned on alcohol and drugs. It would all be a ridiculous cartoon, except the death and horror they sowed was real. On Easter Sunday, 1984, Gary Yarbrough firebombed Seattle's Embassy Theater, an adult cinema. Soon after, Bruce Pierce dynamited the Congregation Ahavath Israel Synagogue in Boise. They slaughtered Alan Berg in June.

Matthews was also planning to murder Henry Kissinger, Senator Bob Packwood, French banking magnate Baron Elie de Rothschild, Chase Manhattan Bank president David Rockefeller, sitcom king Norman Lear. In July 1984, Matthews and 12 men ambushed a Brinks armored car near Ukiah, California. A sign reading "Get Out or Die" was flashed at the terrified guards. They hesitated, and Pierce shattered the windshield with machine-gun fire. In five minutes, Matthews had $3.6 million more to finance his revolution. This time he left behind a trail of clues and clumsy miscues that soon would have hundreds of law enforcement agents on his tail.

He celebrated his victory by passing out gold medallions decorated with the Gaelic inscription "Ye be my battle axe and weapons of war" to men who suddenly seemed more interested in easy money than revolution.

Matthews allegedly shipped hundreds of thousands of dollars to other extremists scattered around the country: $300,000 went to the North Carolina-based White Patriot Party; $250,000 to an extremist named Tom Metzger in southern California, money Metzger would use to recruit skinheads to the Aryan cause; $50,000 to William Pierce, author of the *Turner Diaries*; $40,000 to Butler at Aryan Nations. All but one of these men have denied receiving any money.

The rest of Matthews' money—more than $3 million—has never been recovered.

Using information provided by two corrupt Brinks' supervisors, Matthews planned to blast his way into the company's main vault in San Francisco, where he would steal $30 million—enough, he hoped, to send a tremor through the nation's financial system.

It never came off. In June 1984, Order member Thomas Martinez walked into a Philadelphia liquor store and bought two 50-cent lottery tickets with a phony $10 bill. When he came back the next day and passed another counterfeit bill, the clerk jotted down his car's license number. The Treasury agents who arrested him thought they were on to a third-rate counterfeiter. When they asked him where the bills had come from, Martinez blurted, "You think I want to die?"

Threatened with serious jail time, Martinez agreed to become an informant. Under interrogation, he outlined Matthews' agenda and provided a laundry list of The Order's crimes, a tale that left the FBI, IRS, ATF and Treasury agents gathered around him bug-eyed.

That fall, using information provided by Martinez, FBI agents raided Gary Yarbrough's house near Sandpoint, Idaho. They were met with a fusillade of automatic weapons fire.

Yarbrough escaped into the woods. In the house, they found Yarbrough's wife and children, a disguise kit, a candlelit shrine to Hitler, thousands of dollars and a cache of weapons including night-vision scopes and C-4 plastic explosive. They also found the .45 caliber machine pistol used to murder Alan Berg.

Five weeks later, Martinez directed FBI agents to Portland's Capri Motel, where Matthews and Yarbrough were holed up. From a balcony, Matthews began blasting away at the feds with a pistol; he shot agent Arthur Hensel before escaping, his own hand shattered by a bullet. Yarbrough leaped from the balcony. A dozen federal agents were waiting for him. He was tried on 11 felony charges, convicted and sentenced to serve 25 years. The brooding Matthews ordered Martinez "hunted to the ends of the earth."

At the motel, agents recovered another of Matthews' fevered writings, this one a *Declaration of War*, which read, in part: "All about us the land is dying. Our cities swarm with dusky hordes. Our farms are being seized by usurious leeches and our people are being forced off the land. The capitalists and the communists pick gleefully at our bones while the vile, hook-nosed masters of usury orchestrate our destruction. What is to become of our children in a land such as this? . . ."

Here was corroboration for Martinez's fantastic story. A band of terrorists—a homegrown IRA, if you will—was loose in the West. From Washington, the Justice Department organized a task force of agents and prosecutors to put The Order out of business.

On December 3, Matthews was cornered on Whidbey Island. Four days later, 100 heavily armed lawmen moved onto the island. They evacuated hundreds of residents, rerouted Puget Sound shipping and air traffic. They surrounded two of The Order's safe houses and called on the fugitives to surrender. Even then, the scene had an air of unreality about it. One of the radicals, Randy Duey, burst out of the house at

1749 North Bluff Road, cradling an Israeli machine gun. He looked at the feds ready to blow him away and shouted, "*But you're all white men!*"

One by one, they surrendered, leaving behind stolen cash, automatic weapons, shotguns, pistols, explosives. But Earl Turner had never surrendered. Neither would Bob Matthews. He stayed, cloaked in fantasy, in a house at 3306 Smugglers Cove Road. A negotiating team ran a phone line into the building to reason with Matthews, but the outcome was never in doubt.

Matthews had already written his obituary in a letter to *The Newport Miner* newspaper. "I am proud that we had the courage to stand up and fight for our race. Doing so it is only logical to assume that my days on the planet are rapidly drawing to a close. I will leave knowing that I have made the ultimate sacrifice to secure the future of my children."

Time slowed to a crawl. Tear-gas canisters burst inside the house. Matthews stayed. Twice, assault teams rushed forward and he drove them back. Thirty-six hours later, a helicopter dropped white phosphorous flares on the roof. And the house began to burn. Cradling a machine gun on his wounded arm, Matthews tried to shoot the chopper down. Flames leapt a hundred feet in the air as Matthews ran from window to window, like the hero in a war movie, firing at his tormentors. Then the house exploded.

His remaining men fled, but the task force was ruthlessly efficient. Using the broad powers of the Racketeer-Influenced and Corrupt Organizations (RICO) statutes for the first time in a political case, prosecutors attacked The Order as an "enterprise . . . individuals associated in fact for the purposes of advancing their views of white or Aryan supremacy."

Arrests came quickly. William Nash thought he could hide in an ethnic Philadelphia neighborhood wearing a black cowboy hat and boots. A bartender remembered him as the guy who always left Ku Klux Klan literature in the toilet. Berg triggerman Bruce Pierce, his hair dyed a sickly yellow, walked into a trap in March 1985. Sixty agents were waiting when he showed up at the AAA Answering Service in Rossville, Georgia, to pick up a letter. He was traveling with two machine guns, seven hand grenades, and a pipe bomb. His wife, Julie, arrested in Alabama, was transporting 16 machine guns and rifles, 15 grenades, piles of money and stacks of racist literature.

David Lane was captured later that month outside a Winn-Dixie supermarket in Winston-Salem, North Carolina. Local Klansmen had sheltered him in an abandoned farmhouse. In hiding, writing by candlelight, Lane continued to produce overblown and fantastical treatises on guerrilla tactics: "If in the fortunes of war, a confrontation occurs, remember you cannot afford to engage in a chase scene. ZOG has radios. . . ." In his mind it was all a game right up until the moment he was sentenced to 150 years in prison.

Within weeks of the April 1985 indictment that charged 23 Order members with RICO violations, all but one, Richard Scutari, were in custody. Some had fled to Arkansas hoping to lose themselves in the Ozarks. Three were arrested in the neo-Nazi commune on Arkansas' Bull Shoals Lake where they hoped Jim Ellison would protect them.

When The Order went on trial in September 1985, the Silent Brotherhood proved not so silent. Thirteen of the 23 individuals indicted had negotiated plea bargains and were cooperating with the prosecutors. The trial lasted 14 weeks and cost the government $3 million. The opening-day crowds soon thinned, driven away by numbing barrages of testimony from 370 witnesses. A group of bearded Hassidic Jews dressed in dark suits filed into the courtroom to stare down the anti-Semites. The next day the defendants wore cardboard crosses, but the Hassidim had vanished. Another spectator flashed stiff-armed Nazi salutes. A woman sat mute for five hours, then pulled back a veil. She had a rose clenched between her teeth.

All ten defendants were convicted. Bruce Pierce shouted "Amen!" when his crimes were enumerated. "Whatever I did," he said, "I did to bring honor to myself and glory to my brothers and to God." Pierce and Randy Duey, who killed an Order member-turned-informer named Walter West, were given 100-year sentences.

David Lane asked for asylum in " . . . any white nation that will let us live among our own kind. We will never darken the shores of this continent. Your system doesn't want us and we don't want you. We want to go a place where we don't have homosexuals teaching our kids and our race being mixed." What he got was 180 years in jail.

Gary Yarbrough, the man with the Hitler shrine, drew 60 years. He was led away protesting, "I'm just a common man, worldly dumb but spiritually wise." In March 1986, Richard Scutari, the last of Matthews' original band, was arrested working in a San Antonio brake shop. He was sentenced to 60 years.

If I try to get my message out, you swat me on the head and say, 'Get the heck out of here, you Nazi!' So the blood is on your head.

—Richard Girnt Butler, Aryan Nations

Hayden Lake, Idaho

Robert Matthews is long dead, most of his crazed band locked away until their youth withers. Yet in 12 years their hatred has spread and multiplied like a plague across the land. Paranoid fantasies about ZOG have become truth to thousands of armed patriots and militiamen—men neither as blatant in their aggression as The Order, nor so easily rooted out.

On Rimrock Road in Hayden Lake, the old man lingers. Richard Butler has frozen time. When I arrive, a Leni Riefenstahl tableau awaits me: uniformed storm troopers with bad Hitler haircuts, wolfhounds and red-haired prepubescent girls in white dresses. The 20-acre compound is surrounded by razor wire, a guard tower and sentry post—Butler's own private Auschwitz. A "Whites Only" sign warns the rest of the world to stay out.

Butler hesitates, then invites me into a cramped office. Up close, his face is deeply lined, his eyes a cloudy green. A Philip Morris cigarette dangles from his mouth. Dressed in brown wool pants and a starched tan shirt, working at a metal desk piled high with books, newspaper clippings and correspondence, he looks like a curmudgeon professor forced to teach freshman composition.

"America is in the process of disintegration," he lectures me without much enthusiasm. "What took 500 years to create, we are destroying in 50 years. The frantic effort of ZOG to destroy the genetic structure and culture of our race is proof the end is coming. . . ."

Butler's academic aura is dispelled by the lever-action Winchester and billy club mounted on the wall next to a portrait of Adolf Hitler. Among the books I notice on his desk is a volume titled *Genetic Disorders among the Jewish People.*

"Why are you reading that?" I ask politely.

"For research purposes," he says, squinting through cigarette smoke.

"What are you researching?"

"I would think that's obvious."

A Solidarity Freedom Award lauds Butler "for outstanding patriotic leadership in defense of solidarity for all Christian nations." When I look more closely, I see the award is not signed by Lech Walensa, but one Josef Mlot-Mroz of Salem, Massachusetts, a man who publishes the newspaper *S.O.S.!!! U.S.A. SHIP OF STATE*, whose logo is "All the Patriotic News Suppressed by the Daily Jewish-Controlled Press."

In the early 1970s, I later learned, Mlot-Mroz, who describes himself as a "Polish Patriot tortured by Jew-Communists," assaulted Daniel Ellsburg (the man who publicized the Pentagon Papers) on the steps of a Boston courthouse. In the sixties he confronted a contingent of the Poor Peoples' March on Washington carrying a sign that read, "I am fighting poverty. I work. Have you tried it?"

Butler gives me his own curriculum vitae. In World War II, he served with the Royal Indian Air Force, then the U.S. Army Air Corps. The tragedy of the war, he says, in passing, was the slaughter of millions of white people and the persecution of Adolf Hitler.

In the late forties, he started a company that built precision automotive and aircraft assemblies. He claims to hold the patents for a process used to repair tubeless tires. From 1968 to 1973, he worked for Lockheed as a senior manufacturing engineer. "It was Building 601 in Palmdale, California, where the L-1011 was designed," he tells me. "That was my baby. I set up the final assembly and flight line layouts and installations."

Butler, a big man with a head of silvery hair, then recites his racial pedigree: He is of "German and Scots" background. "Of course, the Scots were Germans, too," he says. "Pierce Butler signed the Declaration of Independence on behalf of North Carolina. There is a shirt-tail relation."

In California, Butler followed Wesley Swift, the rogue Methodist minister who metastasized the benign musings of the 19th-century Anglo-Israelites into Identity theology. "All Jews must be destroyed," Swift wrote.

Swift, eaten up by his hatred, died in 1979, blind and diabetic in a Mexican clinic. Butler and a retired army colonel named William Potter Gale took up the crusade. Gale, tough talking and volatile, stayed in California where he set up a paramilitary militia—much like Bo Gritz, the former Green Beret colonel, is doing today.

Butler moved to Idaho with a small band of followers, choosing to pursue his destiny among the pines and wildflowers, far from the prying eyes of California authorities. As I interview him, he's living in a beige and brown house with his wife Betty and a daughter named Cindy. Another daughter, Bonnie, is living in Lodi, California. Butler's dog is named Von, a mocking tribute to William Von Taggen, the Idaho deputy attorney general who revoked Aryan Nations' tax exempt status as a religious organization.

Charles Tate, father of an Order cop-killer named David Tate, is running the Aryan Nations' printing press, working nonstop to spew out the tracts Butler hopes will spread his message around the world, and maybe bring in cash to keep the good work going. Butler stocks a line of "Aryan Regalia"—arm patches, key chains, belt buckles, hats, even post cards. He says he travels 90,000 miles a year preaching—in his lifeless monotone—to Klansmen, Identity Christians, militiamen, tax protesters.

To Butler, "Robert Matthews is a Patrick Henry, a Nathan

Hale. . . . I don't believe," he says, "American heroes who die, failed."

In 1996, some of Butler's earlier pronouncements seem eerily prophetic: "The government knows people are getting ready," he says. "Training. There are thousands of guns. I see fire and bloodshed. Chastisement. You bet!"

And he sees Jews everywhere. Even in northern Idaho where minorities are practically nonexistent, Butler is obsessed by his hatred. "It's a conspiracy that's been going on for several thousand years," he says, stretching and locking his arms behind his head. "The Jews are doing the will of Satan. Politicians are always telling me, 'We know what you're saying is true, but we don't dare speak out.'"

Excuse me, pastor, which politicians?

"Many, in high places."

"Who, for instance?"

Instead, he rambles on. "The Jew is nothing more than an adversary set up to test our character, will and commitment. The more perceptive Jews realize this. There's a book, *You Gentiles*, by Maurice Samuels. You can feel the author feels the gulf, the split in nature and destiny. It's kind of poignant."

"Really? In what way?"

"It's self-hatred, I suppose."

"You sure?"

"Do I hate Jews?" he says, ignoring me. "I can't hate a thing for what it is. I'm not particularly fond of rattlesnakes, but they have a place here on earth. There's no reason to go out and kill 'em, but they shouldn't be in your bedroom or in the yard with the kids." Butler allows himself a chuckle. "Fortunately, we don't have any Jews, er, rattlesnakes, around here.

"Jews hate me the way they hated the Apostles. The funny thing is, the Jews are coming apart in Israel. You got Orthodox Jews killing unorthodox Jews, burning synagogues." Butler allows himself a chuckle, "Jews are burning Jew synagogues!"

He laughs and laughs.

From the Jews, it's a quick jump to Adolf Hitler. "He is now one of history's monsters," Butler says. "Manufactured by Jewish publishers. When have we had a man, since Leonidas led his Spartans, who stood up for the white race? Who but the Germans fought communism? The Reich was the last gasp of man trying to straighten out the order of things. But the whole world jumped on little Germany, no bigger than Montana, outnumbering them five or six hundred to one.

"Hitler is the most written-about man in history after Christ. I don't care how many people believe Hitler was evil or that six million Jews were slaughtered. The Holocaust is the biggest money-making scam ever invented. They want sympathy and they want power. That's the name of their game."

In the late 1980s, the focus of Butler's Aryan Nations Congress, an annual gathering on the fringe, shifted from survivalist training and rabble-rousing speeches to a more troubling agenda: the literal disengagement from the U.S. government, a psychological repositioning that allows the militias to view their neighbors and coworkers as enemy minions, to see the federal building in Oklahoma City, perhaps, as an outpost of the hated ZOG, a legitimate target in their war.

Seminars on "Forming a Provisional Government . . . Declaring a Territorial Sanctuary" are now part of Richard Butler's agenda. At the traditional cross burning held at one of the Aryan Congress meetings, a Michigan Klansman named Robert Miles, now deceased, set five trash cans ablaze, each supposed to symbolize one of the five northwestern states that will comprise a new Aryan Nation. Dressed in a black robe, Miles shouted, "Hail Victory!" Hundreds in the crowd roared back.

Butler tells me he is embracing a strange bedfellow—Louis Farrakhan—who, he says, will be ceded his own East Coast nation when the United States splinters. "Blacks don't have the same concept of love as we do," says Butler. "You can't apply the same norms to them. Stealing chickens isn't a crime in the mind of a black. It comes naturally. But Louis is trying to elevate that. He's following the law of God more than most white people."

In Coeur D'Alene, not far from Aryan Nations, Father Bill Wassmuth, a Catholic priest who dresses in cowboy boots *and* a clerical collar, is trying to counter Butler's rabid influence. He deflated one Aryan Congress by putting on a Human Rights Celebration a few miles away, a pleasant, sun-washed event crowded with children flying balloons and families eating picnic lunches. A handful of Kootenai County's minorities even showed up.

"To say we live in an area where prejudice is tolerated tortures me," says the tall, handsome priest. "It plays right into Butler's hand. Minorities will not move to a place where they believe goose-stepping Nazis are marching down the streets."

Like Butler's, Wassmuth's words eerily prefigure Oklahoma City, Ruby Ridge, Patriots and Freemen: "Their whites-only nation is an idle dream, but they can make an awful mess trying to make it happen. Somewhere along the line, we'll have The Order all over again."

In 1987, the rectory where Wassmuth lives was bombed by Butler's disciples.

*All I know is Hitler was for the white race. I hear good
things. I hear bad things. I don't care.*

—David Dorr, the Bruders Schweigen Strike Force II

David Dorr stands transfixed in the blood-red light of the
stained glass window. A crowned sword bisected by a Z-like
slash—the Aryan Nations' symbol—is emblazoned on the
glass. The resemblance to a swastika is intentional. A Nazi
battle flag hangs from the pulpit. This church's crucifix is a
huge sword with an Iron Cross on its hilt, the handiwork of a
disciple named Miller "Kymric" Saxon. A portrait of Saint
George and the Dragon hangs on one wall. One of the dragon's horns is topped by the Star of David, the other by a hammer and sickle.

This is the Church of Jesus Christ Christian—a few years
ago, the baptismal font of The Order. David Dorr speaks in
hushed tones, with awe in his voice, as if fearful some Norse
god will send a bolt of lightning to drive him scuttling from the
sanctuary. David Dorr is no Aryan. He is short and dark, with
curly hair and a scraggly beard. A muscular, blue-collar Italian-
American who grew up in San Jose, California. His pastor,
Richard Butler, once considered Italians a pre-Adamic people,
a subhuman race, like blacks, created before God made Aryans
in the Garden of Eden.

But Dorr is a dedicated soldier and therefore useful to
Richard Butler. He's got two black belts in karate and a cache
of weapons and explosives. To Dorr, it's an honor to serve,
without pay, as Richard Girnt Butler's personal bodyguard.

Big-breasted Debi Dorr, dressed in tight jeans and tee-shirt,
also does volunteer work for Butler. In California, she worked
as a guard in a county jail; she's got the shrill voice and combative personality for the job. Blu is their 12-year-old son, a

handsome boy with green eyes and curly hair.

The Dorrs fled California in the mid-seventies, just one step ahead of a muddy tide of Chicanos, Asians and blacks, who they say were polluting the land.

To tens of thousands of Californians, Idaho has become the Promised Land. Most arrive quietly, glorying in the open sky, endless forests, cheap housing. They open small businesses, do their best to gain the grudging acceptance of their taciturn neighbors. An extremist few plunge deeper into the wilderness, with stocks of beans and bullets, determined to avoid whatever holocaust, nuclear or race war, AIDS or some other epidemic, they glimpse on the horizon.

A smaller fraction carry their dysfunction and prejudice with them to a place where there are few minorities to hate or fear. Many seek out Butler's Church of Jesus Christ Christian. A strange congregation: outsiders, misfits, humorless losers eager to blame failure and frustration on dark plots and conspiracies.

The Order was Butler's choir. David Dorr is the last of them. He came too late and missed the killings, the armored-car robberies, the bombings, the glory. His dark eyes register vague disappointment, then brighten. "I'm visible," he tells me, a visitor to his church. "I'm the FBI's target. Someone's got to be out front. I plan on dying to save this place."

His boast is childlike, eager. Over the next few days, it becomes apparent that David Dorr, like the spring drizzle misting the mountains around Coeur D'Alene, doesn't know what he wants to do. One minute he's a hard guy, with a magnum pistol stuffed in his belt; the next, a rock musician who just wants to play his drums. A blue-collar guy who runs bull-dozers and heavy equipment. Friendly and quick to smile, Dorr is eager to be liked. At the same time, he bathes in Butler's grim reflection, parrots the old man's rant.

If pressed, Dorr admits he has trouble following the twists and turns of Butler's mind. Shit, he really doesn't hate anybody. But under the tutelage of Butler, Dorr is discovering the Truth. "Ya know, I used to see a Nazi symbol and say, 'Get that away from me! I don't want nothing to do with that!' Until I found out what it means and what they're about. And what really happened. It took me a long time, maybe a year and a half, to put the pieces together."

We go into town for a few beers, mellow out, exchange life stories.

Back in Butler's office, Debi Dorr jumpstarts the conversation. "Tell him about that guy in town, David. Go 'head, tell him."

"Yeah," says Dorr. "This guy calls me a Nazi. I don't get mad or kick his ass. I say, 'Like wait a minute. What is a Nazi? A Nazi is a nationalist who wants his country to prosper and do good.' Then I ask him, 'Do you believe in marrying a white girl?' And he says, 'Yeah, so what?' I say, 'Do you believe in keeping jobs here in America? Americans making things for American people?' He says, 'Yeah.' And I say, 'Then you're a Nazi!'"

David grins at the beauty of his logic.

Debi is leaning against the office wall, stretching sinuously between the Hitler portrait and the blond, blue-eyed Jesus. "Ya know," she says, shaking her head, "it's these cry-baby Jews. They won't let bygones be bygones. They keep dragging up this Holocaust shit.

"I got into a conflict with these two Jews on a television show. They were fighting for their great-grandfather who happened to have been killed by the Germans. I said, 'If you're gonna carry a grudge this long, you're really sick people. If you can't forgive and forget, go back to Israel and bury yourself. That's where you belong!'"

She tells me about one of the highlights of Butler's annual Aryan Nations Congress: a handful of aged German Nazis show up in their SS uniforms and parade around the compound for a couple of days. "What's the problem!" shrieks Debi. "They're proud of their uniforms and there's no reason they shouldn't be. What's the difference between a bunch of guys at the Elks Club with their little hats with Bullwinkle ears and these guys? You don't see them getting into trouble. It's like, just a bunch of guys! Ya know?"

Dorr snaps to attention. "Hey, I went to school with a kid named Rosenberg. I thought he was a great guy. But now I got Jews calling me up, threatening to gang-bang my wife. The little Jews don't bother me. It's the Rothschilds and the Rockefeller Jews that bother me. Read their Talmud and the *Protocols* and see what they say against us!" (The infamous *Protocols of the Learned Elders of Zion*, an enduring forgery which appeared in the United States in the 1900s, depicts the Jew not just as a religious and social outsider but history's Satanic conspirator.)

Dorr talks and talks. He's a flea-market Nazi who frequents garage sales and second-hand stores, spreading the gospel. "I'm around town all day," he says. "I go to the spa to work out. I meet a lot of people, even lawyers and doctors. I'd say 90 percent of the people around here agree with Pastor Butler. What makes me angry is that the media keeps saying we're un-American and anti-Christian. The people at Aryan Nations are some of the nicest you'll ever meet."

"At first none of our friends knew we were involved in the church," adds Debi. "Now they say, 'If Debi and Dave are involved, there must be something to it, because they are not just off-the-wall jerks.'

"We have their respect. When they ask us questions we say, 'Far out, man!' and sit and rap about it for hours."

Nice is a word David Dorr repeats constantly. Richard Butler is a nice man. So is Gary Yarbrough, the Order member who once came to Debi's assistance when some drunk was hassling her in a bar. The three became good friends until Yarbrough went to jail for killing Alan Berg. "Gary was framed," says David. "'Sides, he could have killed those FBI men who arrested him. That's how good a shot he was."

In California, people were not always nice to David and Debi. "I was born on the east side of San Jose," he says. "My parents pulled me out of second grade because I came home bloody every day. I was the only white boy in a school full of Mexicans. My new clothes would be all ripped up. You can bet my mom was pretty upset."

David's mother still worries about her boy. Back then, she put him in St. John Vianney, an all-white Catholic school. The kids were fine, but now Dorr couldn't deal with his teachers. "I went for eight years," he says. "I learned nothing. Nothing! I hated every minute of it. They force you to do everything their way. You have to believe 'God did this' and 'God's gonna punish you for that.' That can't be right. If God is so good, why is he punishing people all the time? He's gonna send me to Purgatory unless I say 500 Hail Marys and 6,000 Our Fathers because I jerked off. Fuck that!"

In high school, the troubles started all over again. Dorr had Chicano friends ("Bobby Lopez and me used to fight together. Mexicans can take more punishment than anybody."), but the Hispanic gangs took special pleasure in tormenting the short, dark-skinned Italian. "I never used to walk the same way twice," Dorr says. "One day I was walking my girl home from school when 12 greasers jumped me. They beat the shit out of me with two-by-fours and everything. I got them later—one by one—the usual revenge trip. I was only 15 years old, but I knew I had to get away."

Debi was having problems of her own. "I transferred to public school after eight years of Catholic school," she says. "I had to run home and hide under the bed. I was not a violent person. I just wanted to be left alone. My best friend was Filipino. She had to take sides. It was the Chicanos against the Surfers.

"Minority people don't grow mentally," she sighs. "They have a grudge and a chip on their shoulder." Her husband agrees. "If I was down there now, they'd kill me. Mexicans, boat people, niggers, whatever.

"See," he continues, flexing his biceps. "I don't take shit anymore. I got 27 broken bones. I don't mind living with them if they stay on their side of town and don't hassle me. But if I'm driving around and a car pulls up alongside and somebody flips me the bird and says 'Fuck you!' for no reason, I don't like that kind of stuff."

He's determined to spare his son Blu that kind of grief. He's got two other sons from a previous marriage still living in San Jose. He forgets how old they are, but he's sure they're "going through it" every day.

"My parents have an acre in San Jose," he says. "They've got a giant fence all the way around and a fence inside that one. There's guard dogs, burglar alarms and bars on the windows. Even bars on the gardener's cottage. They live in a fort and they think I'm crazy. They don't believe in anything I believe in. They think I'm nuts.

"Up here I can go away and leave my house unlocked. The only people who go through it are the FBI."

Talking like this gets David really worked up. Everyone is beginning to hassle him. The Mexicans have given way to Jews, federal agents, that "fucking priest" Wassmuth.

"Jesus!" says Debi, echoing her husband's thoughts. "You can't even walk down the street anymore wearing a white power tee-shirt!"

David turns to his son, who has been following the conversation big-eyed and nervous. Blu is a husky preteen wearing grass-stained jeans, a sweatshirt and sneakers. A seventh grader with a C average; a star on the wrestling team. He'd rather be outside on his bike popping wheelies.

David: "Blu, what are you gonna do if somebody tries to make us leave Idaho?"

Blu: "Fight."

David: "How hard?"

Blu (softly): "Hard."

Debi beams at the boy. "We're not chickens," she says, her voice rising. "I want my grandchildren to live in a white world. I don't want them to have to breed with other races. That's what they're trying to do. Make it so we can't breed with our kind of people. How can you achieve what you want if you don't fight?"

Debi: "Are you ready to *die* for this, Blu?"

Blu (eyes darting to his father for assurance): "Yes."

Debi (proudly): "He's a crack shot, too."

Blu (trembling): "I want to marry a white girl when I grow up."

Butler has been hovering, troll-like, around the Dorrs, eavesdropping on the conversation. He smiles at the kid, old man's eyes missing the terror. Blu is close to tears.

"He's in transition," says Debi, cradling the boy to her chest. "He doesn't want to die and he doesn't want us to die. He's upset. He understands the possibility we could die tomorrow. . . . All the people we know, their husbands and fathers are in jail. The Order people all came from here and lived around here."

Blu heads for the door, his pain trailing behind him. "We could hide all this from him," Debi says, turning to me. "But this is the truth, something he will be fighting for. I'm his mother. I'm guiding him in what I feel is right. It's not just me. He sees how bad the cops are treating his father."

David Dorr stands once again flexing his bulging muscles, like a nervous boxer about to enter the ring. He pushes against the wall, turns back to the conversation. "I'm telling you it gets real old. The FBI going by our house 40,000 times, questioning our neighbors, sneaking into my motel rooms, going through my papers. In Seattle, I was guarding the pastor. We boarded a plane and I didn't have my gun in a hard case. They arrested me in the middle of the runway. Ain't that trying to provoke me?"

The real question—why doesn't Dorr get the hell away

from Aryan Nations and avoid all these hassles?—goes unanswered. Idaho is big, empty. Twenty-five miles down the road, he, Debi and Blu could live happily ever after in their own blue-collar Valhalla. Dorr's eyes glaze over when I ask the question. He doesn't hear it. Dorr is a junkie; Butler the pusher providing the shot of importance and self-esteem that the little man desperately wants. Like all junkies, David Dorr cannot be reached with words.

In the mid-eighties, Dorr accompanied Butler on a trip to Arkansas, where he visited a 224-acre compound on Bull Shoals Lake that was home to the Covenant, the Sword, the Arm of the Lord. Federal agents put the place out of business in 1985, but "I want to keep it going," Dorr brags. "There's still a lot of people up there who have their shit together and their heads on straight."

He's persuaded himself that thousands of white people in Idaho are preparing for a race war. "We're ready," he says. "Itching for something to happen." He's got food and weapons stashed in the forest in plastic barrels.

"When the time comes," Dorr says, "I see myself in battle, probably one of the leaders. I'm talking about *battle*—when in doubt, kill. That's what it's coming to."

For the moment David and Debi's ire is directed at the Catholic priest Wassmuth, who, they believe, is planning to bring thousands of Vietnamese and Chicanos into northern Idaho. "A lot of people want to get rid of that [Kootenai County Humans Relations] task force," Dorr growls. "We don't want them doing like they did in California. Business owners are downright upset and flat pissed off. If we have to band together to get rid of them we will, no matter what it takes."

Debi walks over and embraces her husband. This Father Wassmuth reminds her of all those bullying Catholic school teachers. "Yeah," she says, kissing David. "Let's go out and get a *petition*. At the next public meeting, we'll slap it in that priest's fucking face."

I leave them standing there. They wave goodbye as I drive under steel gray clouds toward Spokane. There, a floppy-eared black puppy dashes off a porch and runs under the front wheel of my Toyota. I slam on the brakes a second too late. A young woman wails hysterically as the dog, its back broken, dies in her arms. I spend an hour holding her hand, but she is inconsolable.

Four months later, a pipe-bomb, packed with shrapnel, blows out the walls of St. Pius' rectory where Father Wassmuth lives. The priest escapes injury. Nine days after that, three more bombs explode in downtown Coeur D'Alene, damaging a federal building that housed the FBI offices, a fast-food restaurant and a luggage store. A fourth bomb, which did not detonate, is found on the roof of a military recruiting center. Coeur D'Alene Mines, the town's biggest employer, and the *Coeur D'Alene Press* receive death threats. Panic wafts in the autumn air.

Coeur D'Alene, with its fifties-vintage soda fountains and family motels, is dragged roughly into the present. Public buildings are evacuated. Children are pulled out of school by terrified parents. Deputies armed with shotguns patrol the streets.

"This is not Beirut," one resident tells me. "It's goddamn Idaho!" At Aryan Nations, Richard Butler announces the attacks were a ploy "to point the finger at us." He offers a $1,000 reward for information leading to the "capture of the terrorists."

He didn't have to look very far. In the summer of 1987, David and Debi had met Robert Pires, a new-wave racist who modeled himself after Arnold Schwarzenegger's Terminator. Pires, 22, had made the pilgrimage to Hayden Lake from Silver Springs, Maryland, after being scorned by several right-wing groups as too spooky. Pires dressed in black; he wore mirrored sunglasses topped by a spiky haircut that flowed down his back. He kept a Ninja outfit in his rucksack. The Dorrs found him suicidal but *nice*. They let him stay at their house.

On October 6, Pires, a great favorite of Richard Butler, was arrested and charged with the bombing. He confessed, implicating David Dorr and an Aryan Nations' member named Edward Hawley as accomplices. Pires also confessed to the murder of Kenneth Shray, another drifter who had turned up at the Aryan Nations compound. After four months in isolation in the Spokane County jail, Dorr pleaded guilty to counterfeiting charges and was sentenced to six years in prison.

According to the FBI, Pires, Dorr, Hawley and his wife, Olive, were attempting to revive The Order. They called themselves the Bruders Schweigen Strike Force II. Father Bill Wassmuth and members of the humans relations task force were to be their first victims.

"It's all a set-up!" shouts Debi over the telephone, after the arrests and sentencing. "A big bunch of bullshit!" Feisty as ever, she goes into a diatribe against Richard Butler. Isn't it something, she says, the guy remains a free man while dozens of his followers are behind bars. "Hell no, Richard Butler hasn't helped us!" she says bitterly. "He's acting like he doesn't know us!"

As it turned out, Richard Butler would not escape prosecution. In April 1987, Butler and eight other extremists were charged with seditious conspiracy for plotting to overthrow the government. Butler surrendered at the Kootenai County Jail in Coeur D'Alene, where he immediately began complaining of chest pains. He was transferred to a hospital in Spokane, Washington, where he underwent quadruple bypass surgery at the taxpayers' expense. He was eventually acquitted.

Aryan Nations went into a long decline through the rest of the 1980s and into the 1990s. At least 40 of Butler's followers were convicted of crimes ranging from weapons possession to bombings and murder. But Richard Butler's Hitlerite dream is far from dead. In 1994, a revitalized Aryan Nations swept into 15 states, forging alliances with militia groups in the United States and neo-Nazis in Canada and Europe.

The resurgence was due, in part, to the government's 1992

Waco, Texas, debacle with the Branch Davidian sect. The event galvanized extremists around the country.

In 1990, Butler, then 72 years old, had begun courting American and European skinheads. For the last five years he's hosted a youth festival, "a neo-Nazi Woodstock," at the Aryan Nations compound, the last two featuring the popular skinhead band Bound For Glory. He's also been manipulating the media, generating stories in *Spin, Redbook, the New York Times, Inside Edition* and *CNN.*

Butler also forged an alliance with a Nebraska-based neo-Nazi named Gerhard Lauck, whose publication, *The New Order,* has become the bible to thousands of skinheads. In 1994, the tabloid featured a glowing tribute to the Idaho Aryans. Widely circulated across Europe, *The New Order* is printed in German, Dutch, French, Hungarian, Swedish and Danish. Aryan nations all.

What we are seeing in the farm belt is not unlike what happened when Hitler got started.

—Samuel Van Pelt, Nebraska Circuit Court Judge

Chapter 3

A Crisis in the Heartland

*I*t was time to die. The harvest was over in Cairo, Nebraska. Golden mountains of grain mocked the ruined men who had nurtured and coaxed the seed from the soil. Arthur Kirk saw the deputies approaching his house with the paper that would force him off his precious land. He pointed a long-barrelled pistol at one.

"If you don't get off this property, I'm going to fucking blow your head off."

They ran. Kirk knew they'd be back. The arm of the Zionist bankers was long. When the Nebraska State Patrol's SWAT team arrived, he wasn't fooled. It was the Israeli Mossad. Reality flashed in and out of focus, a TV movie watched on a stormy night. He daubed his face with camouflage paint, strapped on a motorcycle helmet and gas mask, then burst out the back door of his farmhouse. Screaming obscenities, he fired wildly at his tormentors. A dangerous, pathetic figure. Two sharpshooters returned fire. Kirk, hit twice, staggered and fell dead.

The police found 27 guns, including an automatic rifle, on Kirk's farm. Scattered among his papers were the antigovernment ravings of the Posse Comitatus. Arthur Kirk owed the banks $302,000. Before picking up his guns, he'd challenged his creditors with an armful of useless lawsuits.

Neither strategy worked, but Arthur Kirk would live on, symbol and warning to thousands of farmers of the government's willingness to use lethal force to collect its debts.

"I worked my ass off for 49 fucking years," Kirk screamed over the telephone before the SWAT team moved in. "I've got nothing to show for it!"

It was a lament every farmer could understand. Within weeks, lurid embellishments of Kirk's death were wired throughout the heartland. In one version, the SWAT team had impaled Kirk's cat against the barn door.

Ten years later, nothing has changed. No one knows how many Arthur Kirks are out there waiting to explode.

Campo, Colorado

Derral Schroder is a big, rawboned man, red-faced and heavy of gut. Suspenders strain to hold up his jeans. A huge L-shaped scar zigzags across his bald head. The pockets of his plaid western shirt bulge with pens, an eyeglass case, sample packets of More cigars. He sits, hunched over a table, surrounded by law books and coffee-stained legal briefs, searching for a way to hold onto his bankrupt farm.

Schroder is preparing a lawsuit, to be filed in U.S. District Court, that will pit him and his wife, Gladys, against the Federal Reserve chairman, the banking system, the U.S. Government itself. His argument, like his situation, is desperate: "Banks create credit out of nothing," Schroder scrawls on a legal pad, "then seize a man's real property to satisfy the debt. This is an illegal, ungodly, unconstitutional act."

It is slow, painful going, the pen an unfamiliar object in his huge, gnarled fist. But Schroder has time to kill. Time to weep, but not to sow. A few miles away, strangers are planting milo (feed grain) and corn on his 3,000 acres; strangers are raping his land. When he drives past his fields and sees the tractors tilling the rich earth, his chest tightens and he wants to cry out. He wants to strike back, but he doesn't know how or where to vent this rage.

It scares Gladys when he gets like this; he's past 60, no kid. The fear she feels is worse than seeing Sheriff Goff and his armed deputies drive over from Springfield and dump a lifetime of her memories—Jesus! Even the children's cribs—out into the road.

Schroder got up at 4:00 A.M. for 40 years, with work to do even before the sun bobbed up orange over the plains. Now the emptiness of these mornings eats at him. Gladys's got a pot of coffee brewing on the stove just like always, the *Today Show* theme still whispers on the television. He catches himself leaning forward to hear the weather report, then realizes it "don't matter if the rains don't come till doomsday."

By 8:00 A.M. he flees the claustrophobic rental house with its flowered sofa, chipped dishes and faded linoleum, and heads over to the old church—not enough folks left in Campo to keep it going—that he turned into the centerpiece of his one great dream: the American Agriculture Movement (AAM).

In the 1970s, AAM roared like a twister out of devastated southeastern Colorado, quickly spreading across the Farm

Belt. "We wanted to make the American people and politicians aware of the plight of the farmer," Schroder says, laughing at his own naiveté.

Back then, the rhetoric was patriotic, not radical; the appeal heartfelt and desperate. Farmers like Schroder wanted justice, not revolution. Parity was the AAM's standard: fair prices for farm products. AAM brought the massive, flag-waving tractorcades to Washington, turning the Capital into a festive county fair. For all the publicity, they failed to stem the tide of despair and misery.

At the church, John Detherage, a hay farmer into the banks for $300,000, is waiting for Schroder. Dale Hyatt, who walked away from his farm when four carloads of deputies showed up and began putting orange tags on his equipment ("I didn't want to hurt nobody"), sits smoking cigarette after cigarette. Both men are in the prime of their lives and have nothing to do.

When Schroder went bust, he was $500,000 in debt, at the time coaxing mountains of grain out of the earth. Now he has no money to hire lawyers. Derral is filing his lawsuit *pro se*, using a prepackaged $400 book of do-it-yourself legal advice that's been circulating around the prairie towns for years. Along with step-by-step instructions, the book explains that a one-world government, controlled by the International Monetary Fund, the Federal Reserve, the Rothschilds and the Rockefellers, is secretly manipulating the farm crisis. This information Schroder and Detherage find easy to believe.

The morning drags on, the whine of tractors plowing distant fields audible in the old church. Derral, smoking, squinting through his reading glasses, works on his brief. Gladys has a friend in Springfield who'll type it up, get it filed with the clerk of the court. Months later, Schroder's arguments will be dismissed as a nuisance lawsuit, one of thousands filed by tax protesters, bankrupt farmers, militia men and patriots clogging the court calendars.

By noon, he's had enough. He limps out to his battered sedan and drives out of the dying town, past the school where attendance has dropped from 200 to 60 students, past Campo's one run-down motel, locked tight. "Call the manager for service," a sign outside reads. But there is no phone.

"It's just a matter of time," says Schroder, turning left and heading out of town, "till weeds grow in the street." A line of tractor trailers rumbles through town, hauling loads north toward Denver. They don't stop.

The land is flat. Wheat fields stretch as far as the eye can see. Schroder's farmhouse is modest—sharecroppers live in more imposing homes—a one-story wood frame structure, white with fading green trim. Surrounding it are sagging sheds, bungalows and a bunk house added over the years as farm and family grew. Now the house is empty and silent. A jack rabbit sits blinking and unconcerned on the front porch.

The buildings huddle under cedar and piñon trees, dwarfed and futile under the empty sky. The wind whistles softly, its currents gently ruffling the grain. Wildflowers and tiny pink cactus blossoms dot the roadside. Birds chirp tunelessly, mechanically in the trees.

Schroder stares. "Three thousand acres," he says. "We grew milo, wheat and corn. We were the biggest broom-corn raisers in the world. I had 27 tractors running all the time, 200-300 people harvesting."

Suddenly, there are tears his eyes. "They're not going to take my land! I produced. I gave society food it didn't have before. I grew it and they won't pay me." The lament is awful to hear, a gusher of hurt erupting from the big, stolid farmer.

A trespasser now, Schroder walks his fields as if dazed. Scattered for a quarter mile in the barrow pit—the strip of land between his fence and the road—are the remnants of a vanished life, a time when he was a proud, prosperous American: rain-damaged furniture, a bedspring, broken equipment, rusted fencing, cattle feeders and a beat-up truck. Forty back-breaking years of struggle and shame, laid out for all to see.

A Baca County sheriff's car slows, then drifts by. A man in sunglasses and a Stetson hat stares at Schroder. The farmer turns, stares back, then spits out the words, "Willard Goff." When Sheriff Goff evicted him two years earlier, Schroder refused, despite Gladys's tears, to haul away his possessions. "Let it be a warning to the rest of the farmers," he told Goff. "This is what happens to us."

The lawman shrugged, signaled to his convict work crew to put the stuff out in the road. What was saved, neighbors took in and stored.

In the 1970s, farming was a growth industry. Schroder borrowed to plant and harvest, eager banks rushed in to subsidize his growth. "I was a millionaire on land alone," he says. "I truly believed you accumulated wealth to disburse to your children and grandchildren." When his son Eugene, a veterinary student, decided to farm, Schroder "made room," borrowing $100,000 to purchase 700 acres for the boy.

Like hundreds of thousands of other farmers, Schroder had forgotten the bitter lessons of the Depression: boom and bust cycles were as predictable as the storms surging across the prairie. In Washington, cattle prices were frozen in an attempt to curb inflation. Beef that should have brought $65 per hundred pounds was barely bringing $34. That same inflation, unchecked in other segments of the economy, sent farmers' fuel, natural gas, seed and equipment costs soaring. Jimmy Carter's decision to embargo grain contracted to the Soviet Union cut across the heartland like a scythe.

Schroder, his life's work vanishing between his fingers, remained a believer. If farmers cried for help, right-thinking folks, whose daily bread came from Schroder bounty, would have to listen.

Nearly one *million* farmers went bankrupt in the 1980s. At the decade's end, those still operating were $200 billion in debt. As the farms died they dragged local banks, food pro- cessing plants, machinery and fertilizer dealers—small-town life itself—with them. In Iowa, more than 5,000 retail stores closed in three years.

And then the pamphlets began appearing at farm auctions and foreclosures, filled with misspelled words and hoary con- spiracies recycled from the Depression. In the eighties, the message grew shrill: *"The Jew plan is to steal your land!"* screamed Klansman Thom Robb in his newsletter.

Looking back, such dislocation was inevitable. In the 1970s, new technologies boosted production and increased exports. Land values soared. Subsidies kept prices artificially high. Schroder, like many farmers, borrowed heavily for new land he planted from pillar to post, eager to take advantage of expanding opportunities. In the 1980s, using those same tech- nologies and cheaper labor, many foreign countries became grain exporters. A strong dollar added to the farmers' woes. And then land values plummeted—40 percent between 1980 and 1986—as markets declined. Collateral disappeared. Men like Schroder who had begun to savor the good life found themselves buried under a mountain of debt. The inefficient failed quickly; by 1990, no one was safe.

By some estimates, 90 million acres—20 percent of the nation's tilled land—was lost to family farmers. As the farms failed, new owners—the government, agribusiness, foreign con- glomerates, the banks—took control.

Schroder and his brother farmers could accept storm and drought, but they could not understand how, in the midst of plenty, they were destroyed. By the early 1980s all of Schroder's land, equipment and cattle were mortgaged. He borrowed desperately, relentlessly. Hearing the rhetoric com- ing out of Washington, he built a gasohol plant to convert surplus grain to fuel. The thing was ugly, dangerous and inefficient, undercapitalized and jerry-rigged. His son Billy was killed in an explosion at the plant. Another dream died.

"Then the bank foreclosed," Schroder says wearily. "I was raising the best crops volume-wise in my life. But the cost of production had went up six times, and we were getting lower prices for our crops than ten years earlier.

"When I was broke, people treated me like dirt. They don't want to associate with you when you was one of the most respected men in the community."

Schroder, who coaxed life from the soil, now imagined himself sowing death and destruction. A man named James Wickstrom drifted into Campo, an organizer for the Posse Comitatus who shouted that the federal government, the IRS, the Jews, were conspiring against the American farmer.

Schroder and his friends listened. Wickstrom soon had them marching across the fallow fields, assaulting shacks, killing some invisible, intangible enemy. The idealism of the AAM gave way to the violent rhetoric of the Farmers' Liberation Army.

On a bitter January morning, Schroder and 250 AAM members gathered at the Baca County Courthouse in Springfield to prevent the court-ordered auction of Jerry Wright's 320-acre wheat farm. Among them was the sixtyish North Dakotan Gordon W. Kahl, a man who would shoot two U.S. marshals to death when they tried to serve him with a warrant. Anger spread from the seething Kahl like prairie fire. Sheriff Willard Goff and county treasurer Thelma Goodnight had become agents of the Zionist Occupation Government that secretly controls America.

"What you gonna do, sheriff?" Schroder shouted.

"I ain't gonna fly south with the geese," answered Goff.

The crowd howled as the papers were read on the courthouse steps, then surged into the building, smashing windows and furniture, engulfing Goff and his deputies. The battle was short and bloody, neighbor against neighbor, using fists, feet, teeth and clubs. Goff, fingers twitching for his riot gun, used Mace and pepper gas to drive the mob back. By then, the courthouse was trashed. And there was no tax base to rebuild it. "We all knew each other," Goff says, "and that made this even sadder.

"This all started as a national effort to strike for fair prices," says Goff. "A good idea. If a man don't want to plant his field, that's his business. But it soon became 'By gosh, you either strike with us or we'll burn down your fields.'"

Now the men of Campo have drifted beyond the pale. Trapped in a forgotten Colorado town, they watch as relentless enemies tighten the noose on their homeland. Another displaced farmer, Van Stafford, tells me he has seen hordes of Vietnamese immigrants settling in Oklahoma "dressed in diamonds and gold braids."

"Who do you think is bringing all the Vietcongs and wetbacks into America?" Stafford shouts, arm crashing into the table where Schroder sits writing. "Why are you seeing a flood of people known to be terrorists? The government gives them $10,000 and guarantees them a job. Look at the Iowa Beef Packing plant in Garden City, Kansas. See how many Vietnamese, Vietcong, wetbacks are working there. See who's paying half their wages and building their houses. If anybody don't believe there's a conspiracy, he hasn't opened his eyes."

On and on it goes, ugly rhetoric spouted under the crocheted American flag in the smoke-filled old church. At the same time, these are men willing to buy a stranger lunch or offer him a place to stay. Ambivalent bigots who'd rather be outside running their tractors and combines.

A few days later, when four of us drive back out to Schroder's farm, the talk in the battered sedan is more of weather conditions than radical solutions. They are uncomfortable with hatred.

Outside, they reach down, their fingers sift the fine soil.

They pull up stalks of wheat to twirl and examine. Derral Schroder, bareheaded, drinks in the wind and sun and soil.

Then he remembers and walks back to the car.

It is not his wheat.

They were gonna run me off and take charge. I never ran in my life. I grew up here.

—Willard E. Goff, Sheriff, Baca County

Vilas, Colorado

Willard Goff is a rangy man, plain-spoken and tough, like the long line of hard men who kept the peace before him. Photographs of his unsmiling predecessors cover the walls of his office, along with the double-barrelled shotgun one of them felt it prudent to carry. Things have changed on the Plains—the Indians and rustlers are gone—but the Law remains. In Baca County, Goff is the Law. "The sheriff has the power," he says, showing off an armful of tattoos. "I have got the stroke."

The law now is not an easy thing. Not like the old days when justice was dispensed quickly with the sheriff's .12 gauge. Failing farmers are dragging Baca County's banks, schools and small businesses down with them. Goff, a struggling farmer himself, is torn. At the grain elevator in Vilas, the sign says winter wheat is selling for $2.40 a bushel, dollars below the cost of production.

He's sitting, sweating in his patrol car in Vilas, a town so dust-blown and dreary that Goff takes a piss on Main Street at high noon without being noticed. In the last three years, he's had to oversee 60 farm foreclosures, a job he has come to dread. The worst, Goff fears, is ahead. "If a man owes for land, machines, and has to borrow to plant and harvest," he says, "there ain't no way in the world he can make his payments.

"A corporation buys his land, they can write off the cost. The small farmer has to pay taxes on the money he makes and still make payments. How can we compete?"

Like Derral Schroder and the others, Goff attended a Posse

Comitatus meeting run by James Wickstrom, hoping for some kind of relief. "They told me the guy would talk on the Constitution," he says. "So I thought I'd give a listen. . . . The guy had blond hair, blue eyes and shiny black shoes. He starts shouting. After about ten words, I'm thinking, 'This sucker's a goddamn Nazi!' Sumbitch knew I was in the back of the hall gritting my teeth. He looked at me and said, 'Do you know what we do when the sheriff doesn't follow the Constitution? *We hang him!*'

"All of a sudden, them farmers started growling. I slap my belt to see if I have my gun. I don't. Wickstrom stood there grinning like he was expecting me to say something. All I could think of was, 'If I blow your brains out, I'll be doing the world a big favor!'

"That meeting was supposed to be the start of the revolution. They were going to ride right over the courts. I said, you ain't gonna change the world fighting with the sheriff. We're neighbors. They didn't hear a word I said. Shit, don't matter if it's me or the president of the United States. They're against government.

"If you're quiet, you're supporting them. Forget me being sheriff. I'd fight these Nazi sons of bitches even if I was John Doe. When they talk about revolution, that means starving my mom and letting my grandkids die. You can bet I won't let that happen."

Next day, Schroder shows up at Goff's office with a box full of audiotapes. The two men listen for a few minutes. Goff hears nothing but ravings against Jews, the IRS, the federal government.

"Derral, them tapes are a bunch of bullshit."

"Willard, we're all starving around here!"

"Derral, as long as I'm sheriff I say we'll starve together."

Goff cuts our talk short. He heads back to Springfield where he must foreclose on another of his neighbor's farms. The tough talk momentarily gives way to a kind of helplessness.

"Listen," he says, "it's my job to enforce the law. But the truth is, I don't know what's gonna happen unless there's some drastic changes."

I headed north. Derral Schroder and Willard Goff stayed behind, tiny figures dancing on the windy plains. Vital men in the grip of forces beyond their control. Neighbors wrenched apart by a thousand ironies. Goff, a free spirit, would follow the law that sustained and defined him. Schroder, whose life had been cyclical and orderly, had come to represent chaos.

If I could, I would hang ten Anglo-Saxons to every Jew. . . . I want everybody to understand that.

—Tom Metzger, White Aryan Resistance,
Fallbrook, California

Chapter 4

Birthing the Skinheads

The beat-up red Cadillac circles the parking lot like a dusty whale. It circles again, more slowly, then pulls up to the Main Street Cafe. Out pops Tom Metzger, a short, stocky, bandy-legged man dressed in tan shorts and sneakers. He looks around warily, a man on a combat patrol in his own town. A blur of tattoos stains his thick, muscular arms. The handshake is quick, almost feminine, then he moves inside the crowded restaurant. If people recognize the man—denounced by the Anti-Defamation League of B'nai

B'rith in 1993 as "America's most notorious hatemonger"—
they don't show it. Except for the can of Mace in a tooled
leather pouch on his belt, Metzger could be any small-town
businessman lining up for the meat-loaf special.

And the ring on his finger. It's massive, a jutting warrior
head set off by a swastika and twin lightning bolts. "It's the
insignia of the Viking Division of the Waffen SS," he says,
holding it in front of my face for inspection. "The swastika
predates Hitler by thousands of years. The thunderbolts are an
Odinist symbol, part of Viking mythology. People don't
understand. This is as old as time."

When I meet him, Metzger, a veteran southern California
Klansman, is hosting a supremacist cable TV show called
"Race and Reason." He's beginning to recruit skinheads and
punks—the working-class whites vainly sought by the New
Left in the sixties—into an organization he names WAR, the
White Aryan Resistance, an immigrant-bashing cadre of storm
troopers he believes has the potential to blow the cities apart.

He's publishing *WAR* and *White Student Union* skinhead
tabloids, running articles titled "AIDS and the Racial Cause," a
column called "Kike Watch," photos of Arnold Schwarzenegger
as the Terminator. A cartoon in one issue depicts a muscular,
Mohawked, drooling Aryan captioned,

> *I'm white, strong and broke and I ain't no goddamned*
> *conservative. The old ways are over. It's open season on*
> *niggers, kikes, cops and capitalists. Kill em all.*

In England, the fascist National Front recruited jobless punk
rockers and skinheads as shock troops in its mid-seventies battles with the Left. Their desperation fed explosive violence.
Now, skinhead bands are winning tens of thousands of fans,
extolling "romantic violence."

Metzger grins, he knows all about them. Over omelets, he
tells me he's grooming his son John to be his ambassador to

the skinheads. "White rage is the key," he tells me. "The key."

He mentions a series of much-publicized shootings and job-related killings, a bloody smear spreading across the country. "It's always a white person either being discriminated against or fired," he says. "Finally they boil over. There are thousands out there, with guns and explosives. Time bombs."

When I interview him Metzger, who still celebrates Anglo victories in the Mexican War, lives with his wife and children on one of Fallbrook's quiet side streets. He says his neighbors are Chicano farm workers. After he set the ground rules—there's a growl of violence in his voice—everybody got along fine. "We have no problems," he says, polishing off his food.

He runs a small electronics business, repairing TVs and VCRs, installing satellite dishes for his increasingly upscale neighbors. "Don't you call me a TV repairman," he says. "I worked five years with Douglass Aircraft. I was with the team that put the first man on the moon."

Lunch over, he announces he'll be back at 5:00 P.M., leaving me the check and five hours to kill on a blistering hot day. Fallbrook, about 45 miles northeast of San Diego, sits pretty among soft rolling hills, terraced orchards and avocado farms. Family operations are giving way to gentlemen farmers, Mercedes slowly replacing the pick-ups on Main Street, boutiques driving out the dry-goods stores.

At 5:00 P.M., the Cadillac bumps back into the cafe parking lot, antennas sprouting like weeds from its roof. Metzger pumps his arm and I follow him to a deserted elementary school parking lot a few miles away. One of his associates walks behind us, cutting me off. We cross a baseball field, its grass wilted in the baking heat, to a solitary picnic table set under a tree. Crude swastikas are carved into the wood. I'm thinking, "Does he hold all his meetings here?"

I zip open my briefcase and reach for my tape recorder and Metzger jumps back, imagining a gun hidden there, eyes bulging in alarm. I hold the machine up for him. We both laugh.

He relaxes, stretches his legs and tells me his story. An only child, he was raised by strict Lutheran parents in the suffocating stillness of Indiana farm country. The same Indiana where Ku Klux Klan membership numbered tens of thousands in the 1920s. A lot of sports and pumping iron could only burn off so much teenage alienation. Metzger was intelligent, but school bored him and his grades reflected it. The endless cycles of planting and harvest, the backbreaking labor, the isolation from the world of action and ideas he imagined on the horizon, triggered one response: *escape.*

After high school, Metzger joined the army and was thrust unwillingly into a suffocating stew of big-city blacks, Puerto Ricans, Chicanos, Filipinos and a rainbow of ethnics that make up the military. Men, he says, who "didn't conform to my idea of what society is all about."

Metzger's accent is surprisingly soft, midwestern, with "ah shucks" inflections that recall the actor Jimmy Stewart. "I'm not a 'nigger-nigger' kind of guy," he tells me. "I wasn't raised that way. I still have a hard time with four-letter words."

Race was the acid that burned into his consciousness. Over time, Metzger would come to believe that his white skin represented both history and destiny. It was the basis for everything he would do and how he lived his life. "Equality is a myth," he says. "A cruel sham foisted by charlatans."

No one incident, he says, engendered such feelings. No physical attack or insult or dark-of-night revelation. "What we are has been determined over millions of years. Some quirk of evolution started white people on a different track. It gave us this heavier frontal lobe. . . ."

I couldn't help but reflect: Every extremist I've met is an amateur anthropologist, and minorities invariably get the short end of the evolutionary stick.

"Tom, can we talk about frontal lobes another time?"

"Not a problem."

Discharged from the military, Metzger drifted back to

Indiana in 1961, and then off again, this time for good. "I was 22," he says. "I jumped into my Austin-Healey with a pair of combat boots, my army field jacket, 150 pounds of barbells and 40 record albums. Away I went, with two feet of snow on the ground, off to California."

He married a woman named Kathleen. Metzger, like the millions of other working-class Americans, struggled to raise a family that quickly expanded to six children.

In the sixties, Metzger followed other conservative Californians into the Republican Party. He campaigned for Ronald Reagan in his first gubernatorial bid, went all out for Barry Goldwater in 1964. From Goldwater, it was a quick step rightward into the John Birch Society, which, Metzger says, was "ostensibly not a racist organization, but the majority of people in it were racists."

In the late sixties, Metzger, shocked by the bloodshed in Vietnam, took an antiwar stance and was consequently kicked out of the Birchers. What he saw happening in Vietnam made him a virulent anticapitalist. "I began to wise up," he says. "They had no intention of winning, so the hell with it! Why get innocent guys butchered?"

He protested by refusing to pay taxes, a move that quickly got him into a nasty tangle with the IRS. "I had two TV repair stores, people working for me," he says. "Was my goal in life to spend 40 years selling stupid televisions? Is that what I'm here for? They bury me and say, 'Oh he was a good business-man.' That wasn't me.

"I moved my business onto my property where I could guard it. I got with the Posse Comitatus. The IRS tried to seize my house. Nine treasury agents came out to hand me a piece of paper. The guy's hand was shaking so much he could hardly hold it. I was right on the edge, a real time bomb. It's a won-der I didn't get killed."

In the middle of this, Metzger converted to Catholicism, embracing the Latin Mass and traditional ritual just as the church was becoming more liberal. His kids were in parochial school when he joined the Klan. "Hey, all kinds of Klansmen are Catholic." Now he says many Catholics, adrift and uncertain within the church, are hearing the call of Identity Christianity."

He brought new and riotous life to the Klan. The image of Klansmen as brutal, night-riding bogeymen, he decided, was all wrong for the seventies. Metzger imagined forward-looking racists who could handle ideas as adeptly as axe handles. He was issue oriented. Affirmative action and immigration affected all white people. He'd use the media—the burning cross is a TV news staple—to get his message out.

He picked his shots carefully. At nearby Camp Pendleton, white marines clashed with black troops in 1978. The white soldiers were disciplined then shipped out incommunicado. Furious, Metzger held a protest march on the base. "These were things they never could have gotten away with with blacks." He says he even convinced the San Diego ACLU to support him. The Los Angeles ACLU was defending the black marines. "It caused a real big split," Metzger says.

A fund-raiser in Oxnard, California—he screened *Birth of a Nation*—turned into a bloody confrontation with the communist Progressive Labor Party, whose members showed up in protest. "We caught 'em off guard," remembers Metzger, whose men wore black uniforms and carried shields. "We got in that hall and the communists just went crazy. The funny thing was, they started beating the hell out of the cops instead of us."

Metzger savors his street battles with leftists, blacks, cops, the Jewish Defense League, as if they were real victories. In his newspapers, he likes to run blurry pictures of himself in the middle of these mêlées.

In the mid-1980s, Metzger and Louisiana Klansman David Duke wound up on a border tour under the auspices of the Immigration and Naturalization Service. "We got in a helicopter near San Diego and came down right on the border in the middle of a group of reporters. Hell, it was just a $30 flight.

"That copter coming out of the clouds and the dirt blowing, and all the reporters scattering. It was beautiful." He held a press conference to announce the "KKK Border Watch." Metzger got what he wanted: reams of newsreel footage and glaring publicity. "People started thinking more and more about that border."

In 1980, he ran for Congress. Whites were beginning to respond to David Duke's messages about aliens, affirmative action, minority crime and declining job opportunities. Metzger won the Democratic nomination in California's 43rd District, polling more than 32,000 votes in one of the state's most populous districts. His Democratic opponents had split the vote, allowing Metzger to win—a candidate who dressed in sheets and burned a cross outside the state capital in Sacramento.

He lost the general election to a veteran Republican, learning a lesson, he says, about trying to work within the system. "I thought there might be a possibility for evolutionary change. Maybe I could do some good. I had lots of gut issues: crime, welfare and all that. I had some good answers, too, but they never made the newspapers. All they wanted to talk about was 'Klansman . . . Klansman . . . Klansman.'"

Metzger eventually quit the KKK, the way he'd quit the Catholic, and later, the Identity Church. "I don't believe in God," he tells me. "I don't believe in the Divine Right of Kings or the Divine Right of the capitalist system." Things had changed so much that he supported Jimmy Carter ("a lot more justice oriented") against Ronald Reagan.

He says the Klan is a conservative, pro-America organization, wanting to enforce the law of the land. "Back then I was 'Mr. Support Your Local Police.'" But the crap the cops pulled—breaking agreements, sending in snitches—culminated in a riot where Metzger says he almost got killed. "A riot during a congressional primary. Not too many candidates can say that.

"You know, I began to have a hell of a lot more compassion for what these blacks were going through. That's the oddest thing. While a Klansman, I began to appreciate the struggles of others. I saw how frustrating it can be to try to accomplish something legally. Ronald Reagan to me was the most dangerous man in America."

A rapprochement with Louis Farrakhan again piggybacked Metzger into the national spotlight. Metzger relishes the story. He put out feelers and was invited to a Farrakhan rally in Los Angeles. He sat surrounded by "20,000 blacks," no easy thing for a man who believes African-Americans are "recreating transplanted jungles in the inner cities." When the moment came, one of Metzger's flunkies marched up and put $100 in the collection plate. "Those blacks were cheering the White Aryan Resistance. How you gonna match that?"

As he speaks, a formation of C-130 military transports circle, then move into a landing pattern over a nearby military base. "Here they come," Metzger says bitterly. "They can't wait to get into another war. Millions died in World War II, a big chunk of them were white. Then Korea and Vietnam. The cream of our race thrown into the garbage grinder."

Metzger is hard to pigeonhole, easy to underestimate. His mid-eighties opposition to American involvement in Central America was in line with the views of his liberal enemies. The same is true for his tough stand on civil liberties and ecology. His heroes are Jack London and the old labor organizers, the Wobblies of the twenties.

"People on the left," he says, "are usually sharper than those on the right."

A white separatist, he is frustrated by his own people. "How can nature understand a race that kills 15 million of its own with abortion?" he asks. "How can nature respect a race that consumes, gorges and, when it overproduces, goes to war?

"You know," he says, "I consider anybody who opposes me

my enemy. I don't care if they have blond hair, blue eyes or what. If I could, I'd hang ten Anglo-Saxons to every Jew. There are more white traitors in this country than there are Jews. I want everybody to understand that."

Evening is approaching. His buddy has not returned to pick him up in the Cadillac, a serious breach of security. So I drop Tom Metzger by the side of the road. He walks off, a bandy-legged guy in polyester shorts and shirt.

I head back down the long, sweeping curves of Highway 76 to the coast, and then north toward Los Angeles. California is golden under the setting sun, the ocean peaceful. Metzger's alien notions, his latest gambit with the skinheads—I'd witnessed their violence firsthand in London—pound in my head. I try to shake them. I never notice the roadblock until I'm right on it. Refrigerator-white vans and massive spotlights clog the highway. The Immigration and Naturalization Service is hunting illegal aliens.

The agent peers at my white face, grins and waves me on into the night.

Metzger's outreach to the skinheads would bear bitter fruit. In the late 1980s, he began manipulating all-too-eager radio and TV talk-show hosts into offering him guest appearances, providing, in effect, widely disseminated propaganda he could never otherwise afford. In 1988, Tom and his son John and a group of their skinhead supporters were involved in a televised mêlée on "Geraldo." Rivera's nose was broken when someone hit him with a chair.

That year, Metzger wrote a letter to a Portland, Oregon, skinhead gang, East Side White Pride, which read, in part, ". . . Soon you will meet Dave Mazzella, our national vice-president, who will be in Portland to teach you how we operate and to help you understand more about WAR. . . ."

On November 12, 1988, members of East Side White Pride attacked three Ethiopian immigrants with baseball bats and steel-toed boots, killing one, Mulugeta Seraw. Three gang members were convicted of Seraw's murder. Investigators looking into the case turned up the gang's links to Metzger's organization.

Dave Mazzella, who was not charged in the murder, later testified that Metzger said "the only way to get respect from skinheads is to teach them how to commit violence against Jews, Hispanics, any minority. The word will spread and they'll know our group is one you can respect."

Mazzella was a key witness in a civil lawsuit brought against the Metzgers by the Southern Poverty Law Center and the Anti-Defamation League (ADL) on behalf of Seraw's family. In October 1990, an Oregon jury rendered a $12.5 million judgment against Tom and John Metzger.

Tom Metzger found himself owing $3 million; John, $4 million. Another $5 million was supposed to come from WAR's assets. The judgment was upheld on appeal on April 20, 1993. According to the ADL, it was one of the largest civil verdicts of its kind in U.S. history.

Tom Metzger was also tried and convicted for his part in a 1983 cross-burning incident in Los Angeles. His sentence was commuted after 46 days so he could be with his terminally ill wife, who died in March 1992.

Metzger's home and other assets were seized as a result of the civil judgment. Any revenues accruing to him are being monitored by the courts, but it is unlikely that the award will ever be paid off. The intended chilling effect on Metzger's operations has not taken place. White Aryan Resistance hot lines are still humming.

In the aftermath of the 1992 Los Angeles riots, Metzger's hot line carried this message: "The courts and the police, along with our keepers in Washington, are corrupt to the core. . . . Any attack on that system that weakens Big Brother is fine with white separatists. . . . Too bad they didn't take out city hall and the federal building. . . ."

Lynn, one of his daughters, runs the Aryan Women's League, an organization described in WAR's newsletter as "trying to recruit White racially conscious women to battle the Jew/mud/Zombie/Mutant/degenerate lesbos."

In 1996, Metzger seized upon the Waco, Texas, assault as proof of the federal government's intention to stifle its patriot opposition. He was out there again pounding the angry drumbeat that has raged in his blood for 30 years.

It's all . . . it's all . . . conspiracies.

—Joyce Dimmit, Posse Comitatus

Chapter 5

The Posse Comitatus

Johnson, Kansas

The Posse Comitatus (the phrase is Latin for "power of the county") harks back to medieval English Common Law. In this country, a posse, familiar from a thousand TV westerns, represents the able-bodied men in any county who can be summoned by a sheriff to preserve order. The "Christian Posse," dreamed up in the 1950s by a washing-machine salesman from Oregon named Henry Beach, is something else.

The county, Beach argued, is the seat of all government. It

followed that the duly-elected sheriff, not the U.S. president or Congress, was the only lawful authority, a notion that had some interesting corollaries: Unless authorized by the Constitution, all federal and state laws are unenforceable. The Federal Reserve Act is unlawful. Mortgages are invalid instruments of usury. Gold and silver are the only real currency.

Beach, a member of the Silver Shirts (a fascist paramilitary group) in the thirties, and later the far-right Minutemen in the sixties, saw conspiracies everywhere. Nelson Rockefeller, he once predicted, would be appointed national dictator. His followers predicted the same. In February 1983, one of Beach's disciples, Gordon Kahl, was convinced Hitler and the Jews had conspired to fake the Holocaust.

Forerunners of today's militias, the posses sprouted like weeds through the 1980s. Beach couldn't sell enough $6 badges and $21 charters. His disciple James Wickstrom set up a Posse township in Tigerton Dells, Wisconsin. He claimed arrest powers, kept a jail, even issued citations for traffic violations.

Next came threats against IRS agents and judges, the armed men walking down Tigerton's main streets with pistols strapped to their belts, the rattle of automatic weapons from the nearby hills, the roadblocks manned by Posse members. Wickstrom ran for governor, failed, then declared himself Tigerton's judge. Eventually, he was jailed for impersonating a public official. Wickstrom traveled the country wearing a blue beret with a skull and crossbones flash, urging farmers to follow Wisconsin's lead. It was he who threatened to hang Sheriff Willard Goff in Colorado.

By the mid-1990s, Wickstrom, released from prison after serving time for counterfeiting, was up to his old tricks, this time as an Identity Christian linked to the militia movement. He had a 900 number he called "Fed-Up American" that spewed hate at $2 a minute, and he shared a post office box in Noxon, Montana, the base camp for the Militia of Montana.

Posse members wear gold pins in the shape of a hangman's

noose in their lapels, a reminder of Henry Beach's command that uncooperative sheriffs are to be "removed by the posse to the most populated intersection of streets and at high noon, be hung by the neck."

In Johnson, Kansas, I spent a couple of days with a septuagenarian named Joyce Dimmit and a 39-year-old auctioneer named Jim Carrithers, a man whose business card declared him "the Selling Sound of the Southwest." Both were lifetime residents of the tiny west Kansas community, and both were Posse Comitatus sympathizers. Carrithers supplemented his income selling real estate and pizza out of a storefront off Johnson's main street.

Sitting on her shady front porch on a hot summer afternoon, Dimmit tells me about her grandparents, who arrived in Kansas in a covered wagon. A street in town is named after her grandfather, one of Johnson's mayors. Freckled and green-eyed, Dimmit was educated in a one-room schoolhouse. She spent 50 years working alongside her husband, "raising kids and running machinery." Talk to her and it soon becomes clear she stands against anything that chips away at individual rights, a living throwback to frontier days. Her father had even opposed consolidating the draughty, one-room schoolhouses run by each community into a county system. He'd resisted every bond issue, every tax initiative—terrified he'd lose his land and cattle to satisfy other men's debts. His fears have come to life in his daughter.

In debt for $400,000, she lost her 1,400-acre wheat farm when the Federal Land Bank foreclosed a few years back. "I don't have property," she says, "and I don't exist."

A grandmother who should be looking back on a full life and ahead to retirement, Dimmit is brimming with bitterness. "All my life I drove tractors and milked cows," she says. "I done all the usual things, had my kids in 4-H and the Boy Scouts like everybody else. . . .

"Till we found out." In the 1980s, Dimmit began listening to the speeches of the Posse organizers who floated through town like tumbleweed. She nodded in agreement in the grange halls, her anger and despair feeding the rage of her neighbors. "I began to learn about the Council on Foreign Relations, the Trilateral Commission, the Federal Emergency Management Administration," Dimmit says. She enunciates the awkward titles carefully, as if the words were diabolical incantations.

"People began to inform us farmers that these things existed. Things we'd never been touched with or concerned about. . . . We were lied to in school. The schools are set up to lead people in the wrong direction so you don't learn the truth. They teach sex education and all this immoral stuff. Teenagers are stealing, drinking, committing suicide."

Who is behind these plots?

"This is all stemmed from the Vatican," she tells me, her mouth twisting as she spits out the words.

"The Vatican?"

"It's all run from the Vatican," she says again. "The Vatican is the one-world religion. The Jews and the Jesuits have a big part."

"Joyce, you know, I'm Catholic and I've never heard. . . ."

"Then you best get off my porch. Got no more to say. . . ." She gets up and moves toward the door of her house, her back stiff with anger. She turns around to me as I'm backing down the porch steps.

"You really want to see a Hellacost!" she says. "Go back to when you Catholics were murdering your own people in the Spanish Inquisition. We're all going back under another Inquisition."

The door slams behind her.

Jim Carrithers is a big confident man, a former high school athlete who dresses in jeans and plaid western shirts. He's still married to Firma, his high school sweetheart, and he loves her dearly. Trying to provide a good life for her and their three pretty teenage daughters keeps him running.

"You bet I'm a workaholic," he says as he strolls into his crowded pizza parlor to check on noonday business.

Carrithers tells me he has just won the title World Champion Auctioneer in a national competition.

"That's a pretty elite group," he adds, punching me on my arm.

Yet in Jim's clear, resonant voice, there is rancor. And behind that, deep-seated, seemingly irrational fear. Phrases like "starving to death" pepper his conversation as he drinks a Diet Coke in his restaurant. He tells me a story. On a bright Sunday morning in 1982, he and two men walked into county sheriff Jim Garrison's office "humble as could be."

Carrithers had discovered that in the event of an emergency or war, FEMA, the despised Federal Emergency Management Administration, was planning to relocate the populations of Wichita, Denver and Kansas City into his western Kansas backyard.

Irrational as the notion was, Carrithers couldn't sleep. He was tormented by the thought of "millions of hungry people" invading his hometown, hurting his wife and kids. "People," he says, "who would kill you for a hamburger."

Carrithers asked Garrison to help set up a Posse Comitatus in Stanton County. He gave the sheriff a load of Posse literature and the audiotapes that had so outraged Sheriff Willard Goff in Colorado. Garrison listened politely, and, when the delegation left, he pulled out a file on a Posse gathering that had taken place in Wesken, Kansas. The meeting had been described as a three-day "Ecological Seminar: To Clean Up This Land of Ours." It turned out that budding ecologists were given sniper training, taught bomb-rigging and guerrilla warfare.

Garrison alerted the state attorney general, and soon enough Carrithers' patriotic plans were crushed by lawmen threatening to throw him in jail for conspiracy.

"Conspiracy!" he snorts. "You bet there's a conspiracy under-way. *They* will control everything. Everybody will be a pauper, working and performing for the international bankers."

He walks outside his pizza joint, sweat beading across his fore-head.

"When they come at me with a gun, I will die fighting. If I don't fight for my family and my freedom, God is not going to think very much of me."

And then he's gone, off to try and track down an errant load of pizza sauce and relishes he figures he'll need for the scout meeting and Little League games this evening.

The Posse is a way for citizens to get organized when the government gets out of hand.

—Kenyon Koefed, Posse Comitatus

Soda Springs, Idaho

I arrive in Soda Springs, Idaho, still searching for the Posse Comitatus. I find a town whose phosphorous mines are shutting down, where failure hangs in the air palpable as the stench of processing plants. In a dingy downtown cafe, a farmer sipping coffee tells me two months of dry weather have wiped out his barley crop. "We had five inches of rain on Saturday," he grunts. "One drop every five inches."

A big American flag flies above the town park. A late-afternoon Little League game, Mountain Bell against Monsanto, is under way. Three generations of townspeople fill the stands. Among them, a row of prepubescent girls who whoop and holler for their hero, a waif no more than 60 pounds. The players—Travis, Zach, Derek—are too skinny to fill out the corporate logos on their tee-shirts. Mountain Bell wins on a long triple, hit by a graceful, blond kid.

The girls scream even louder, the rival coach whacks his hat against his thigh in disgust. When the hero discards his batting helmet, long blond curls tumble out: a girl. There are handshakes and ice pops for all. The crowd disperses, home to dinner, an early turn-in. Tomorrow's a work day.

A souring economy is not only threatening Soda Springs' jobs; its way of life is at risk. Unemployment is driving families away, the tax base and school enrollment are eroding. One day, I know, the baseball games will stop.

In the sixties, the John Birch Society had taken root in the community, stirring people up about the threat of communism and New Left radicals. Now, according to the Posse Comitatus, the enemy was no longer lurking behind the Iron Curtain. In the eighties, a group of Soda Springs' debt-ridden ranchers and mine workers, led by Cliff Turner, formed a Posse to protect, as they put it, citizens "from encroachment by any part of government in violation of constitutional guarantees."

In Soda Springs, Cliff Turner and a red-haired firebrand named Kenyon Koefed raged against everything from oppressive taxation to sex education. In plain English, that meant keeping IRS agents, collectors of *Satan's tithe*, out of town. They found hundreds of workers and ranchers willing to listen, and soon the Posse took on a burgeoning life of its own. At its peak, the Soda Springs Posse totaled 300 men led, says Koefed, "by former Green Berets and army officers."

Furious town meetings set friends and families against one another, shattering the tranquil Mormon community. Turner ordered his children to march into elementary school singing a song, "Cut the Thieving Hands Off the IRS." It was as if a fever had swept through Soda Springs; no one knew how long it would last or what the outcome would be. Posse members threw away their drivers' licenses and ripped the plates off their cars right in front of law officers. Signs were posted on the county line: *Federal Agents Keep Out: Survivors Will Be Prosecuted.*

Trying to head off trouble, the sheriff, a cautious man named Richard Weaver, refused to let IRS agents into Caribou County unless their papers were in scrupulous order. "He was being very careful," says Koefed. "He didn't want a war on his hands, and it could have very easily come to that. We were armed to the teeth."

Declaring himself the Posse's "Special Prosecutor," Turner issued citizens arrest warrants and "Wanted" posters with Weaver's face plastered on them. He dared the sheriff to stop him. "I'll have a shoot-out with you," Turner promised.

It was the state, not the feds, that cracked down on the rebels. A judge ordered Cliff Turner and a dozen of his lieutenants incarcerated until they provided information on their taxable assets. Turner refused and was thrown into the county jail he claimed he owned as a Posse leader. He waited for tough-talking Koefed to break him out.

And waited.

Ironically, it was those small-town verities I'd witnessed on the baseball diamond that kept Soda Springs from exploding. Koefed was no crazed radical or preening storm trooper. He worked in the Monsanto plant and hoped one day to become a manager. Not all his friends and coworkers agreed with the Posse's stand, and that ate at him. He was an elder in the Mormon church, an officer in the army reserves. He had a wife, Suzanne, and three children to think about.

Their photos sit on a battered piano next to a book of hymns in the living room of his modest home. Koefed hands the pictures carefully to me, then smiles as I make over his attractive family. "The Posse could have gone in there and broken them [Turner and others] out of jail," Koefed says, replacing the photos. "There was no way the sheriff could have kept them, not with our numbers. We could have taken our county—no sweat. But it would have been neighbor against neighbor. I didn't want that. And I realized, neither did Sheriff Weaver. I was the Posse commander. I couldn't allow killing."

He hesitates. "We lost," he shrugs. "The economy got even worse, and now we're completely disorganized.

"Hey, I'm sorry. You want something to eat?" He offers me a bologna sandwich slathered with mayonnaise.

Koefed says that after months of protests and hunger strikes, a tactic they'd picked up watching the civil-rights protests of the sixties, the rebels gave in. Cliff Turner, sparrow thin and half-delirious, disappeared into the mountains, eventually settling in a place so high up—the farmer drinking coffee in the downtown cafe told me—"when he pissed off his porch it fell 6,000 feet."

Hell's Canyon, Turner's redoubt, straddles the Idaho-Oregon border, south of Lewiston and Clarkston. I drove south on deserted Highway 195 looking for Grangeville, the closest town.

Something slammed into my windshield hard. I saw a flash of red, and then through the rear-view mirror, a cardinal fluttering helplessly in the road.

"Jesus!" I backed up the car. The broken bird skittered and thrashed into the underbrush quickly beyond the reach of mercy.

In Grangeville, Sheriff Randy Baldwin thought it hilarious that I had driven all this way looking for Cliff Turner; the guy had moved away. "Hey buddy," Baldwin said, "you want crazies? We got all you need." His silver front tooth flashed as he and Deputy Gene Meinen regaled me with stories of smugglers of automatic weapons, drug-lab operators and other rascals who were killing each other so regularly in his peaceful-looking county, it "saved us shooting them." He told me I'd find Turner in flat, grassy Fenn, an Idaho town with a population of 49.

After five tries, I reach Turner by phone. A suspicious man, he finally agrees to meet me at 5:00 P.M. and gives me a jumble of directions. He mumbles something about having business to take care of. It's barely noon. I spend a long afternoon reading about gold miners, railroad men and Indian wars in back issues of the *Idaho Country Free Press*, a newspaper that had been founded by an Englishman a hundred years earlier. I share the deserted library with a blond, freckled boy about 13, dressed in jeans and a ragged tee-shirt. He studies furiously for hours, frowning over big words, then sounding them out and moving on to the next sentence.

Fenn, Idaho

Fenn is a town with one store and a rusted-out grain elevator. Cliff Turner pulls up in a faded sedan, gets out to shake my hand. He's tall and gangly, with a dramatically cleft chin, thin, slicked-backed hair, and long sideburns, a 55-year-old trapped in an awkward, adolescent body. Dressed in brown pants baggy enough for two people, white plastic suspenders, zippered Beatle boots, white socks and a loud tie, he's preposterous. Then I realize he has put on his best clothes to greet me.

We drive back to his house together. He's got pieces of tissue plastered on his face where he cut himself shaving. The back seat of the car is stacked with piles of *pro se* legal instruments, allowing him to function as his own lawyer. If he's pulled over by the police, Turner files barrages of lawsuits, demands a jury trial for a traffic violation, which is a daunting undertaking for a small town.

His home is faded and green, a converted store or filling station, I can't tell. Flies buzz in the late afternoon heat. The furniture is mismatched and lumpy, flea-market scraps. He tells me he cuts timber, does some hauling, sells an occasional tract or anti-tax audiotape through the mail to support himself. "I could have been rich," he says, swinging his ten-year-old step-daughter in the air, "but I'd rather be free."

Trisha, Turner's pig-tailed, gap-toothed third wife, nods in agreement. She's a hard-core survivalist who was living with her two daughters, Shona and Lesa, in a cave in the Grand Canyon "without no electricity, no water, looking for a simple life." She read one of Turner's anti-tax fliers, and the two began corresponding. After a few letters he sent her a bus ticket. Two days after she arrived in Soda Springs, they were married. That was nine years ago. A lesson to twice-divorced me.

Shona and Lesa are home-schooled with second-hand textbooks and a curriculum provided by the Christian Liberty Academy. "Thank Yahweh for that," says Turner. He's a member of an obscure religious sect, based around Fenn, called the Name Believers, or Elijah's Message, who decry the use of the words *God, Jesus* and *Allah* to identify a supreme being. From what I can gather there are no congregations, no churches—only small tabernacles in believers' homes.

"The school superintendent came by here," continues Turner,

"and said, 'I understand your girls ain't coming to school.'

"I said, 'They ain't gonna be there neither. You better come out here with your guns. I can teach 'em better by far.'"

The girls are shy, skittish as fawns. They look at me as if I'd climbed out of a spaceship. "What about friends, clubs, sports, Girl Scouts?" I ask. "Don't you want them to have that?"

"I grew up without social interaction," he says. "I turned out just fine. Just fine."

Obviously, I'm thinking.

Clifford E. Turner was born near Soda Springs in a community where half the people were his cousins, uncles or aunts. His great-grandmother, a midwife, delivered a thousand babies in the town. As a boy, he spent most of the year working the family farm and, as a result, never got past the eighth grade. "I was a long, skinny, gangly beanpole," he tells me, flopping on his couch. "The target for all the teasing and making fun of. By the time I left school, the fun had been picked out of me."

Then came an epiphany. "One day," he says, "four guys were beating the tar out of me. Along came this big high school senior and banged their heads together. *He defended me.* All my life I've remembered that. I became the Fonzie of my day. Younger kids came to me for help. I'd beat the tar out of bullies. Even with the colored. I'd stick up for them when they were picked on."

He earned his GED in the army; returned to Soda Springs, where he took a job in the phosphate mines; then emigrated to California for a few years, where he worked on the assembly line in a Ford plant. He resented the hard-eyed managers looking over his shoulder, trying to squeeze more work out of him. He read Orwell's 1984 and saw it was Big Brother breathing down his neck, spying on people, poking into their personal business, stealing what they earned with their sweat. "I realized the IRS was simply another bully, scaring the devil out of people. I did some studying. The IRS had no constitutional authority. It was simply a big bluff.

"To see little people being harassed and destroyed made me mad."

He moved back to Soda Springs. A flirtation with the John Birch Society ended when he found their "endless conspiracies worthless." Turner, involved in a successful battle against sex education in Idaho schools, ran for governor, but nobody noticed. Then he decided to go after the IRS for financing "the killing of unborn babies." The anti-tax foundation of the Posse Comitatus was the perfect vehicle. He began traveling around the country, "a hick from a small town who visited 42 states," preaching the gospel. "The Posse represents the people's right to protect themselves from tyrants," he says. "Be they motorcycle gangs or government hoodlums. All I did was ask the sheriff to protect our county from thieves who were operating in our area: IRS agents."

It's hard to imagine a scarecrow like Turner leading a band of armed insurgents. "I couldn't rob a bank," he says. "I'd drive ten miles to repay 25 cents when I'm over-changed. It just makes me mad to see a government that's more dishonest than any of its citizens."

In his travels Turner came across fellow Posse organizer Gordon Kahl, a farmer who had been a tail gunner on a bomber in World War II. Kahl, a grandfather then in his sixties, was, in critical ways, Turner's polar opposite. His hatred of the federal government, of Jews, of the IRS, was visceral.

"I can't find anywhere in the Constitution that only white people have rights," says Turner. "Talk about race turns me off."

Kahl was always armed—to the point of carrying his Ruger Mini-14 semi-automatic rifle with him to church. And he was violent. In the seventies, he was convicted of income tax evasion, sentenced to a year in prison and five years' probation. Released, Kahl ignored the terms of his probation—as he'd refused to file his taxes—and instead traveled the country recruiting farmers and rabble-rousing for the Posse.

In 1983, federal authorities decided to crack down. On February 13, Kahl, his son Yorie and two other Posse members attended a meeting—Kahl would later write that it was to organize a "third Continental Congress . . . to restore the power and prestige of the U.S. Constitution"—at a clinic run by a Dr. Clarence Martin in Medina, North Dakota.

Driving north on Route 30, Kahl and his party ran into a roadblock at the top of a hill. As he pulled over, other police vehicles roared up from behind, sealing any escape. For a long moment, half a dozen armed men on both sides of the law stood staring.

Someone fired. Yorie Kahl was hit in the stomach. Kahl opened up with the deadly little mini-14, hitting U.S. marshal Robert Cheshire in the chest.

"You hit bad?" screamed a deputy as Cheshire fell.

"No, not bad," said Cheshire.

A minute later he was dead, the high-velocity bullet lodged in his flak jacket had shattered his thorax. Blasting away, Kahl killed another marshal, Kenneth Muir, and wounded two other law officers.

He talked gently to the wounded men, then helped Yorie back to his car and drove him to Dr. Martin's clinic. He stood there as the dead and wounded were carried in.

"Was it worth it?" one of the wounded men moaned.

"To me it was," Kahl said, then disappeared into the fog on the dark side of the Continental Divide.

Four months later, he was trapped—surrounded by hundreds of law-enforcement agents—in a farmhouse converted into a fortified bunker in the Ozarks.

Lawrence County sheriff Gene Matthews, 38, a giant of a man who had walked into the farmhouse trying to persuade Kahl to surrender peacefully, instead took a bullet in his chest. He bled to death on the farmhouse floor. In the ensuing battle, the house, packed with thousands of rounds of ammunition, exploded and burned. Like Robert Matthews, Kahl remained inside, firing away.

Gordon Kahl became the far right's first martyr, an inspiration still to today's militiamen and patriots. At the Aryan Nations compound in Idaho he was awarded the "Aryan Medal of Honor Second Class," for "a most outstanding example of Christian patriotism and in the best tradition of American resistance to tyranny."

Cliff Turner has taken another path. He's got a 60-acre "farm-stead" back in the hills stocked with food, weapons, a horse and a mule. Enough, he says, to keep him, Trisha and the girls alive for years.

"There's ten kitchens in Mexico that will feed 10,000 troops each," he whispers as he drives me back to my car. "You gotta be ready. Any man who knows what I now know would be a fool not to prepare."

As I leave him, I sense that, unlike Kahl, Turner has won his battle. There's nothing for the cops, the tax men, anybody, to grab onto. He's free, part of the prairie, as taxable as a stone or a tree stump.

I race the setting sun out of Fenn, roller-coastering over hills and rocky canyons, plunging into shadowed valleys and back into blinding sunlight. The land, part of the Nez Perce tribal reservation, is wild and desolate, monumental in scale, beautiful in a barren, painful way. No roads, no construction, no development marred the place.

The road sweeps out of the highlands and parallels the Salmon River. I pull over to clear my head and walk to the bank. Slate-gray water rushes by with hypnotic force. No ripple betrays the power of the stream. I have to pull back or get sucked in. Living in such untamed places made freedom visceral. Treacherous. These canyons would never be taxed or tallied, licensed or limited. Storm and drought were unpredictable and ungovernable.

I made Ontario, California, the next day, then drove west to Burns. A man selling homemade pies by the side of the road pleaded with me to make a $1.50 purchase. His eight-year-old daughter played in the dirt as I sat on a car fender eating crumbling slices of boysenberry pie. I was seeing more and more of America, an America far from the coasts and centers of gravity.

This America seemed a country of poor people. Everything was for sale right there in the front yards, faded memories and broken dreams recycled like polyester clothes and cheap cassette players. I'd driven a thousand miles without seeing a BMW or Mercedes. I saw dented Chevys parked in front of laundromats and convenience stores. In Utah, I stood on a corner and watched a pimply teenager drive endlessly up and down the deserted "strip" in a souped-up Dodge Charger, forlorn and displaced as his 1968 car.

In the desert south of Burns, scattered homesteads were named Poverty Ranch and Last Chance without a trace of irony. A turquoise lake shimmered like a mirage in the distance. As I got closer, I realized no boats or cabins lined the shore, vegetation near the water was dead, the few trees burned gray-black. Away from the water, grass and shrubs were stunted or dying. Lake Albert was alkaline, and lifeless.

Fierce winds whipped a poisonous spray onto the roadway, shaking my car. Lightning flashed against the basalt cliffs that rimmed the lake. I drove on and spent the night in a dilapidated motel in Goose Lake run by Hindus who'd been expelled from Idi Amin's Uganda. All the other motels in town displayed garish "American-Owned and Operated" signs. I was sick of this shit. The manager's lonely young wife, unhappy in an arranged marriage, separated from her extended family, told me that an American man had spat on her two days ago as she and her mother-in-law shopped in a farmers' market.

"Why did he do that?" she asked. "We have not harmed him."

"I don't know," I mumbled. But I did.

I'll blow your fucking head off!

—Slim Parrino, Ministry of Christ Church

Chapter 6

The Italian in Me

Mariposa, California

Next morning, I wound through the Cascade Mountains into Redding, California, where I picked up Interstate 5. From there I drove south then west, looking to catch up with William Potter Gale in Mariposa, California.

Gale, a retired army colonel, was a seminal figure on the far right, a self-confessed hatemonger and anti-Semite who constantly fomented violence. "The Bible says to hate with a perfect hatred," Gale liked to say. "The preachers have been lying about the Bible. They're preaching love, love, love."

Old and in poor health, Gale ran the Ministry of Christ Church out of a double-wide trailer on a barren desert tract he called Manasseh Ranch. He was a bitter rival of Aryan Nations' Richard Butler; the two fought for disciples as if there weren't enough hate in the world to go around. Gale had organized one of the earliest posses, a paramilitary group he called the California Rangers.

I pop a cassette into my Toyota's tape player, a recording of one of Gale's sermons, "Victory with Jesus," broadcast over KTTL, a radio station in Dodge City, Kansas.

". . . Yes, we're going to cleanse our land," Gale rants. "We're going to do it with a sword. And were going to do it with violence! 'Oh,' they say, 'Reverend Gale, you're teaching violence.' Damn right I'm teaching violence! God said you're going to do it that way, and it's about time somebody is telling you to get violent, whitey!

"You better start making dossiers, names, addresses, phone numbers, car license numbers, on every damn Jew rabbi in this land! And you better start doing it now. And know where he is. If you have to be told any more than that, you're too damn dumb to bother with! You get these roadblock locations, where you can set up ambushes, and get it all working now. . . ."

I wanted him.

Gale came from an old military family. His father had supposedly been one of Teddy Roosevelt's Rough Riders. Gale ran guerrilla units in the Philippines during World War II and claimed he was promoted to lieutenant colonel at 26, a full decade ahead of his army cohorts. "I killed Japs," he bragged. "Plenty of them with a knife."

Battlefield injuries kept Gale hospitalized for many months after the war, eventually forcing him into retirement. He read the Bible as if it was ongoing military history. Twisted by war and pain, he embraced Wesley Swift's Identity Christian beliefs, which made Jews, blacks and struggling Chicanos the enemy. "I'm a peaceful man," Gale liked to say. "I'd rather play golf, but the Jews won't let me. They tell damn lies about me!"

As early as 1965, the California state attorney general denounced Gale's heavily armed Rangers "as a threat to the peace and security of our state."

Over the phone, I try to cajole his wife, Roxanne, into granting an interview.

"Definitely not," she says.

I drive on.

Aimed south, I plunge into the baking heat of the San Joaquin Valley, arriving in Merced, then head east to the foothills of the Sierra Nevada. Mariposa, a historic gold-rush town, is the gateway to Yosemite National Park.

Tired, determined to get this interview, I swear under my breath, then decide: I'll just show up.

It's late afternoon when I arrive. The National Headquarters of the Ministry of Christ Church squats in the middle of an unpaved, unmarked road, miles outside town. The gate is locked, the guardhouse protecting the property empty. No one responds to my repeated horn blasts. I start to climb the fence, then catch myself.

"Don't be stupid." I'm not thinking clearly.

I drive through a rabbit warren of side roads, finally stopping for gas at a dilapidated country store. The proprietor, his flabby arms a blur of faded U.S. Navy tattoos, watches me dial Gale's number. The phone rings once, twice.

"Ministry of Christ Church," a male voice, wary.

I identify myself. "I'd like to speak to Pastor Gale."

"He's out of town."

"For how long?"

"Indefinitely."

"Please, I've just driven 500 miles to do an interview. Is there someone else I can talk to?"

Pause. "Try Slim Parrino. He's the assistant pastor."

"Perrino?" An Italian? I hang up, grab the battered

Mariposa phone book. Perrino . . . Perino . . . Perrina? There's no listing!

The "sailor" is standing beside me.

"You want Slim *Parrino?*" he says, pointing out the window. "It's the second driveway on the left."

"Thanks, buddy."

I rocket across Darrah Road and up a steep gravel driveway. A tan and brown house sits at the top. A pick-up truck is parked outside. Good, he's home. I turn off the engine. I'm halfway out of the car when two big dogs, fangs bared, hurl themselves at me. The first crashes into the car door, knocking me backward across the front seats. I try to grab the dashboard for balance. The gearshift lever jams into my spine.

A moment later, the passenger door is jerked open. A crazed man—I see the corded veins in his neck popping—rams a long-barrelled pistol into my face.

"WHO THE FUCK ARE YOU?" he screams.

"Ah. . . ." I'm paralyzed, speechless, staring at him upside down. The man cocks the silvered pistol. I close my eyes.

Parrino twists the gun barrel against my cheek, hurting me. "THE FUCK ARE YOU?"

I try to say something.

"YOU GOT TWO MINUTES TO GET OFF MY PROPERTY!"

He slams the passenger door and comes around to the driver's side, gun pointed through the windshield at me. On the porch, a third dog is tearing at its chain, choking, trying to get at me.

"I'LL BLOW YOUR FUCKING HEAD OFF!"

Hands shaking, I start the car, back up and head down the driveway spewing gravel. Parrino follows me, holding the pistol steady with two hands.

I swerve back into the gas station. I sit there, eyes darting to the rear-view mirror, trying to steady myself. The sailor is outside pumping gas into a station wagon.

"That guy's a goddamn maniac," I gasp.

"We got a few of them around here," he says.

As I drive off, I feel the pump jockey's eyes on me. I look back in the mirror. The bastard's laughing.

A day later, a newspaper reporter tells me about Connie Hammerly. I find her standing in the middle of Highway 49. She's a flagman, dressed in a hard hat and tight faded jeans, detouring cars around construction along the roadway. Connie is attractive with startling blue eyes. She asks me if I can wait until she takes a lunch break. Then we'll talk. I wait, watching every man who passes smile or flirt with her. Finally, she walks over to her car, takes out a thermos, unwraps a cheese sandwich and some fruit. She puts a big cassette player on the hood; it whispers Bible passages.

Connie tells me that she, her husband, Frank, and their three children followed Gale from the Los Angeles area in the late seventies. Frank, a construction worker, was hooked on Identity Christianity. Connie had her doubts.

"I was raised that God is love," she says. "That's not what Gale was teaching. Frank was hearing what he needed to hear: He could blame other people for his failures."

After a year she split, taking the kids with her, preferring poverty and loneliness, she says, to the ugliness of Gale's ministry. A lifetime later, her kids now grown, she is still struggling. Her three children are charismatic Christians, one a Bible scholar, she says, working on a kibbutz in Israel. She's very proud.

As we speak, another son, 25-year-old Jeff, and a friend drive up in a yellow VW Beetle. I notice a fish, the symbol for Christ, plastered on the bug's engine lid. Jeff, with his long hair, beard and beer gut, looks more like a Hell's Angel than an apostle. His friend, a paper-thin, scraggly blond, has what looks like a knife scar running down the side of his face. The guys have brought Connie a blueberry muffin for dessert.

When Connie introduces me, the blond sneers, refuses to shake my hand.

"Don't talk with him, Connie," he says. "He'll make trouble for you. Mess up your job or something."

"What are you talking about, man?"

He looks at me. "Ain't no story around here. You reporters like to hurt people and go on your way."

"That's not true," I say, still thinking of Parrino.

"Bull!" The guy spits the word out, walks back to the VW. I notice he's got bad teeth, a gimpy leg.

"Don't mind him, man," Jeff tells me. "He's cool."

Jeff was nine years old when his parents joined William Potter Gale's congregation. He played cowboy, explorer, Indian fighter; rode horses on Gale's 95-acre ranch. In the church trailer, he mumbled half-understood prayers and drowsed during Gale's sermons while his father glared at him. After the divorce, his mother introduced him to another Christianity.

"When I got older," Jeff says, "I started following the Word. The Word and what Gale is saying are two different things. He takes the Bible and distorts it. 'If you ain't white, you ain't right.' That's the message. They think they can be good Christians and piss on everyone else.

"'We're the Twelve Tribes,'" he mimics. "'And you ain't shit!'"

He sits on the car hood, sipping a beer beside his mother. The bombing in Oklahoma City is years away, the militias just stirring in the heartland.

"These people are not harmless," Jeff says. "I've known them my whole life. I'm like 'em in a lot of ways. Not much school . . . not too many prospects. Trying to get a decent job, raise a family. It's real tough out here."

"They ain't harmless, man," he adds. "And they're getting worse."

I weighed 300 pounds and it didn't show. No one is going to fuck with me. I'll bust their ass.

—Paul Paige, Mariposa County sheriff

I decide to hang around town hoping for Gale to return. Still wary of Parrino, I seek out Paul Paige, a former Mariposa County sheriff who has had some dealings with him. I find Paige at home, standing in the shade of a mulberry tree feeding hummingbirds with an eyedropper filled with sugar water. The man is huge, the birds no bigger than his thumbnail. I'm six feet tall, weigh 200 pounds; next to him I feel like a little boy.

An enormous gold and silver belt buckle holds up jeans big as spinnaker sails. Before I finish introducing myself, Paige shakes my hand, leads me on to his porch and bangs a jug of homemade wine on the table. He pours and shoves a glass into my hand.

"Have a drink," he says and lights a big cigar.

Mariposa is no radical hotbed, he tells me, but a town where people come to raise their children, "a good place with good folks, even if the damn population has qua-tripled." When he was sheriff, the occasional outlaw gang came through, but Paige and his buddy Reid Marks, who shows up in the middle of our conversation, were always able to handle them with consideration and common sense. Failing that, they resorted to baseball bats.

"Right, buddy?" says Paige.

"Fuckin' A."

"William Gale," he says dismissively, "is an opportunist who attracts people, gets what he wants and unloads them. Shit," Paige continues, "the old bastard's sickly, henpecked, even his dentures are bothering him."

"Sumbitch gonna die soon anyhow." That from Marks.

When Gale's threats attracted the attention of the FBI and ATF, Paige and one of his deputies snuck up to the ranch one night looking for illegal weapons and explosives. "We tore the place apart," he says. "All we found were shell casings." Gale's "church" was packed with sophisticated recording equipment.

"The guy was shipping out 80 tapes a week," Paige says. "At ten dollars a tape. Not too shabby."

As the afternoon wears on, Paige's preposterously entertaining stories about Hell's Angels' conventions and hippie orgies in Yosemite give way to a meditation on the nation's well-being. "Gale is a thing of the past," he tells me, draping his arm around my shoulder. "You're Italian. I'm a Kraut. What the fuck is the difference? We all from someplace else.

"We ain't got a perfect government, but we got a darn good government. Society is imperfect, but you think Gale and his kind are going to straighten it out?"

"Bull . . . shit," says Marks.

"You always gonna have radical bastards," Paige continues. "They ain't gonna do nothing. They start shooting people, they're gonna get slaughtered."

Paul Paige and Fortunato "Slim" Parrino grew up in Canoga Park outside Los Angeles, blue-collar kids looking to bootstrap themselves up by becoming police officers. Like many immigrants, Parrino, a shoemaker's son, rejected those who came after him, those, perhaps, too much like himself. Instead, he fell under Gale's Aryan spell. Working as a deputy sheriff in the Malibu substation, Parrino got himself in trouble when, per Gale's exhortation, he began using law-enforcement computers to compile dossiers on his "enemies."

A few years later, he followed Paige up to Mariposa, where he tried to catch on as a deputy sheriff. "He took the test," Paige says with a wink, "but rated low because of his attitude." Parrino held Paige responsible for the rejection.

"Slim got angry," says Paige, "but not that angry. I weighed

300 pounds and it didn't show. I'm the sheriff of the county. No one is going to fuck with me. I'll bust their ass!"

Instead, Parrino bided his time and ran against Paige for the sheriff's job—campaigning on the Posse Comitatus platform. "He said I was too liberal," laughs Paige. "We shouldn't be listening to federal and state authorities. He wanted to take over the sheriff's office and tell everybody to go to hell. . . . He got ten percent of the vote."

I stir in my chair. Many hours have gone by.

"Where you going?"

"Paul, it's almost 9:00 p.m. I've got to find a hotel."

I'm getting drunk, too.

"Stick around. My wife's Italian. She made you spaghetti."

Next thing I know, he's dragging his ancient mother-in-law, black dress, gold crucifix and all, in front of me.

"She's from the Old Country. Go ahead, talk to her."

"Paul, I don't speak Italian."

"Don't matter. Talk to her. I think she's bored."

After a huge dinner and much more wine, he pulls out an antique Mariposa County deputy badge, hands it to me.

"Take it, give it to your daughter. Go 'head."

"Paul, I can't."

"Go ahead!"

Then he pulls a cloth drawstring bag from a drawer. It's filled with gold nuggets he's panned from local streams.

"Come on, take any one you want. For your daughter, not for you. I collect 'em. Take that one, it's a good one."

"Paul, I can't." He stuffs the nugget into my shirt pocket and sends me, staggering, on my way.

For all his strength and hard-core decency, I later realize Paige, like so many Americans, is naive, even innocent. And he's wrong about the threat. When the bomb goes off in Oklahoma City and those awful images crash through my television screen, I think of him, helpless as the rest of us.

Next morning, I drive to Uncle Joe's in Lush Meadows, a restaurant that sits a few hundred yards from William Gale's home. "Uncle Joe" and Audrey Noel are hyphenated Americans, the kind of folk Gale despises. Joe's father was a French-Canadian from Quebec, his mother Irish and English. Audrey is an Italian-American who grew up near San Francisco.

Married 35 years, the two had always struggled. Joe, a navy veteran, hauled freight, worked construction, pumped gas, drove the Mariposa school bus, before opening the restaurant. His nose is squashed like a pepper and he's got a big waxed mustache. With his red shirt and pants, he looks vaguely like a circus clown. Audrey, like so many of the Italian-American women I grew up around in Brooklyn, has a heart of gold, but you don't want to mess with her.

Over coffee, Audrey, her eyes magnified behind huge eyeglasses, picks up Paige's story of Slim Parrino's campaign for sheriff.

"He walked in here one day and said, 'You need my help.'

"I said, 'You son of a bitch, if I needed your help, I'd kill myself. I don't believe in what you're doing, so don't preach to me.'"

"'You'll change your mind when I'm elected.'"

"The day you're elected, I'll leave town!"

"'You'll have to.'"

Paige creamed Parrino in the election.

The next night I'm sitting in the mostly empty restaurant when Gale—I recognize his face from newspaper photos—walks in. He's got about a dozen men, dressed in jeans, plaid shirts, poplin jackets, with him. Fortunately, no Slim Parrino.

They sit at a long table, talking softly as they wait to order beer and soft drinks. Uncle Joe is passing out menus—the cuisine runs to pizza and submarine sandwiches—when one of the guys leans back. A revolver falls out of his jacket pocket and clatters to the floor. The guy reaches down to pick it up, but Joe sees it.

"You know you can't have that in here!"

"It's my right!" the gunman snarls.

In a moment Audrey is on him, a barrage of foul language cutting the guy like a knife. When Gale stands up to protest, she turns on him.

"Fuck you, Gale!"

"You ain't a Christian," Gale splutters. "You ain't even white. You're Italian!"

"What are you?"

"I'm an American."

"So am I," says Joe. "So is she!

"All of you, get the hell out of here! Goddamn it, I mean it! Check the guns or get the hell out. Now!"

The men shuffle out. Gale is the last to leave. He turns back toward me for a moment. Our eyes lock and then he's out the door. Next day, I try calling him. Once more, he's unavailable.

A few months later, Gale and six others are charged in a ten-count federal indictment, alleging, among other things, that they conspired to execute judges, peace officers and federal agents.

The group had founded yet another revolutionary organization, the Committee of the States, a name taken from the Articles of Confederation. The Articles had preceded the U.S. Constitution and called for a committee of the state to run the nation.

According to the indictment, Gale and the others also set up an "Unorganized Militia" which engaged in paramilitary training "in daytime ambushes, night time ambushes, knife fighting, garroting and other offensive maneuvers. The ideological indoctrination included comments by defendant William P. Gale on the need to kill Internal Revenue Service agents and other public officials. . . ."

In 1988, Gale and three others were convicted and sentenced to a year's incarceration. Justice was served.

William Potter Gale died in prison.

We're not the haters of Negroes. The haters are the politicians who say to the Negro, 'You can't do it without our help.' Personally, I don't think they can do it either. But let's give 'em an opportunity. In Africa."

—Thom Robb, KKK leader

Chapter 7

The Klansman's Daughter

ogged by rattling thunderstorms, I cross the plains of Texas and Oklahoma into Fort Smith, Arkansas, then head north and east into the fog-shrouded vastness of the Ozarks. Economic war is raging in the mountains. Tenth-generation natives are scratching out a living on chicken farms, their children swallowed up in the gigantic soul-sucking warehouses of Wal-Mart and Mass Merchandisers, Inc. Hordes of loud-talking, free-spending vacationers and snowbirds from Cleveland and Chicago are fueling a boom in retirement and vacation homes. Pristine mountain lakes are being developed into family recreation centers. The landed gentry is getting rich selling off its patrimony; the poor make do hawking hillbilly cooking and shoddy mountain crafts.

The weather has cleared, the evening sky ablaze with stars. I spend a restful night at the Ozark Inn ("Good Sanctuary for Christian Travelers"). In the morning, the radio is honking a Saturday livestock auction in Decatur, Arkansas, every hog and heifer brought squealing or lowing into the pen described in the kind of detail one hears on the runways of Karl Lagerfeld and other couturiers.

Limosuin cows are bringing in $60 per hundred pounds, a sum drastically reduced—just like the rag trade—by wormy coats. I wonder when the Ozark Inn will broaden its appeal, when live-stock auctions will give way to easy listening. The Ozarks, 60,000 square miles of rolling mountains and bright streams, will change. One of America's remaining virgin territories will eventually be ravaged.

Like the Cascades and northern Rockies in the Pacific Northwest, the Ozarks are also survivalist heaven. Southern Missouri and northern Arkansas comprise the so-called Mo-Ark (as in Noah's Ark) region, the safe haven that will shelter them from the Armageddon and racial conflagrations that are to purge America. For years, they've gathered in ragged communes, religious cults and paramilitary camps. Tiny groups with big, scary-sounding names: The Christian Patriots Defense League; the Covenant, the Sword, the Arm of the Lord; Elohim City; the Save America Gun Club; the Women's Survival Corps, the KKK; and the Nazis. They are all here, the violence-prone and the peaceful, swallowed up by the mountains, just beyond the crash of the bulldozer clearing next year's housing tracts.

Caricature of ZOG, the Zionist Occupation Government, as depicted in the tabloid WAR (White American Resistance).

FOR ACTIVE CHRISTIAN-PATRIOTS ONLY!!

C.S.A. NATIONAL CONVOCATION

★ Christian ★ Identity ★ Patriotic ★ Survival

OCT. 8, 9, 10, 1982 — FREE Admission — Secluded

To Be Held on the Secluded 224-Acre CSA Property in Pontiac, Missouri

Primitive Camping Facilities available on property
or you can stay at one of the nearby resorts in Pontiac.

Guest Speakers: Col. Jack Mohr (Ret. US Army)
Bob Miles (Mountain Church)
Richard Butler (Aryan Nations)

Plus CSA's own instructors and other outside teachers! There will also be an open forum time for people to speak. PLUS the establishment of a National CSA Confederacy.

Informational and Participational Classes include:

Weapons	Income Tax	Health	Betrayal of America
Wilderness Survival	Shooting Weapons	Racial Truths	The Jews
Christian Army	Food Storage	Natural Childbirth at Home	
First Aid	Personal Home Defense	Self-Defense	Rappelling
Nuclear Survival	AND MUCH, MUCH MORE! ! !		

Facilities include classroom areas, shooting range, and our own "Silhouette City" for Military Training.

PRE-REGISTRATION is Required!! Only White, Patriotic, Serious CHRISTIANS need apply.

For Attendance Registration Form or for information, please write or call:

the Covenant
the Sword
the Arm of the Lord

C.S.A. ENTERPRISES
RT. 1, BOX 128
PONTIAC, MO. 65729
501-431-8882

Plan To Attend!

Announcement of national C.S.A. convention, appearing in C.S.A. Journal.

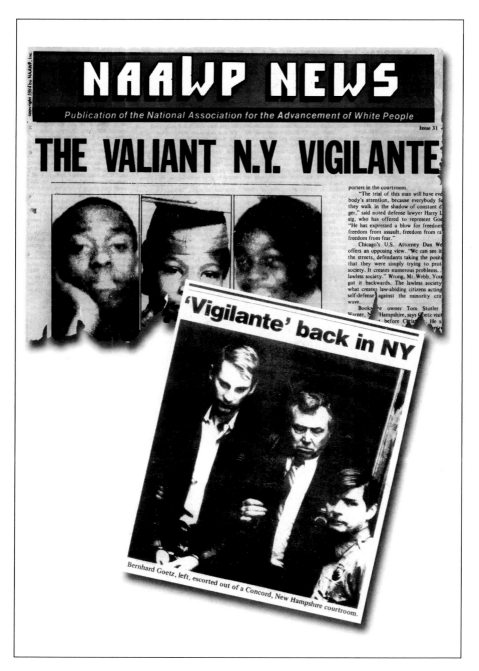

NAAWP News celebrates vigilante Bernhard Goetz.

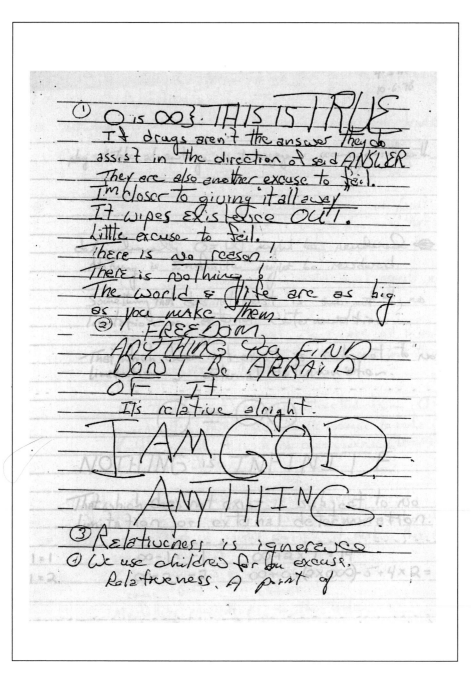

① O is ∞③. THIS IS TRUE
It drugs aren't the answer they do
assist in the direction of said ANSWER
They are also another excuse to fail.
I'm closer to giving "it all away"
It wipes existence OUT.
Little excuse to fail.
there is no reason!
There is nothing.
The world & life are as big
as you make them
② FREEDOM
ANYTHING you FIND
DON'T Be AFRAiD
OF IT
It's relative alright.
I AM GOD.
ANYTHING
③ Relativeness is ignorance
④ We use children for an excuse.
Relativeness. A part of

A page from the diary of schoolhouse bomber David Young.

Front flap of Aryan Nations brochure, with depiction of Aryan "warrior."

Political cartoon from The Confederate Leader.

THE FUTURE BELONGS TO THE FEW OF US STILL WILLING TO GET OUR HANDS DIRTY.

POLITICAL TERROR

It's the Only Thing They Understand.

NSLF Headquarters
P.O. Box 61
Kenner, LA 70063 U.S.A.

build the

WHITE REVOLUTION

through

armed struggle

THE PROTOCOLS OF THE LEARNED ELDERS OF ZION

AN OUTLINE

Introduction

The Protocols of the Learned Elders of Zion were discovered at the turn of the century by a brilliant student of editorial research, Victor Marsden. Marsden, while a correspondent for the London Morning Post in Russia was thrown in jail and expected to be assassinated. By a miracle he escaped with his life and vowed that the first thing he would do would be to translate a document he had discovered (The Protocols of the Learned Elders of Zion). It was Mr. Marsden's belief that The Protocols were issued at the first Zionist Congress held in Basle, Switzerland in 1897, under the Presidency of the father of modern Jewish Zionism, the late Theodore Herzl.

This deadly document contains 24 Protocols made up of 283 articles. Every paragraph is sensational and shocking beyond the ability of the average reader to believe.

The quotations which follow are accurate examples.

1.

PROOFS OF IDENTITY!

(Answers the question "Who are God's Chosen People?")

by
BRIG. GEN. JACK MOHR, C.P.D.F.
(Lt. Col., U.S. Army, Ret.)
113 Ballentine St.,
Bay St. Louis, MS 39520
(601)467-4415

"If ye will know the truth, the truth will set you free."
(John 8:32)

"Let The High Praise Of God
Be In Their Mouth,

And A Twoedged Sword
In Their Hand"
Ps. 149:6

ARYAN NATIONS

Church of Jesus Christ Christian

P.O. Box 362
Hayden Lake, Idaho 83835

Pastor R. G. Butler

TO OUR NEW PEOPLE:

Thank you for contacting us and for your interest in Aryan
Nations.

Enclosed is a sample packet of introductory literature on Aryan
Nations. Several additional complimentary mailings will be
forthcoming.

We sincerely hope that you will see the importance of our mission and
join with us as a member or a supporter. Our yearly subscription
rate is $15.00, which entitles you to our monthly magazine newspaper
and our semi-monthly special newsletter.

If we do not hear from you after several months your name will be
removed from our mailing list.

Remember, the survival of the White Race depends on what we do
now!

Yours for Faith, Race and Nation,

Richard G. Butler, Pastor

Solicitation letter from Pastor Richard Butler of Aryan Nations.

Yesterday: the Tribes of Israel

DENMARK

SWEDEN

NORWAY

U.S.A.

FINLAND

GREAT BRITAIN

GERMANY

ICELAND

FRANCE

SPAIN

ITALY

HOLLAND

N

ASHER   DAN   NAPHTALI

THE HOLY ORDER

NUM. 2:2-34

LEVITES

PRIESTS   TABERNACLE   PRIESTS

LEVITES

REV. 21:9-27

SIMEON   REUBEN   GAD

S

W   E

BENJAMIN EPHRAIM MANASSEH

ISSACHAR JUDAH ZEBULUN

Today: the Aryan Nations

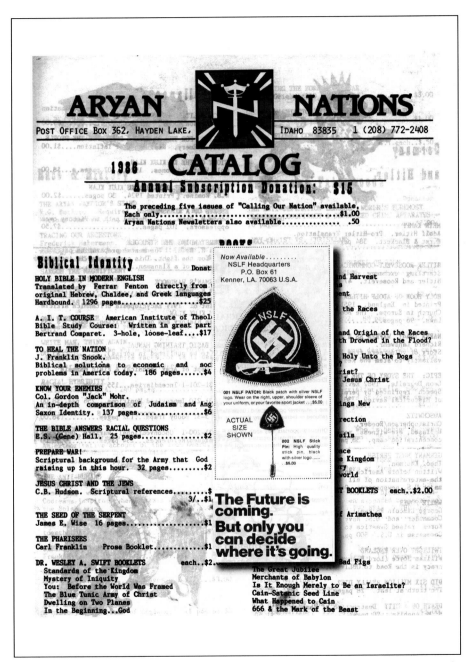

Books, tapes, posters and pins available.

Gordon Kahl and David Lane: martyrs to the cause.

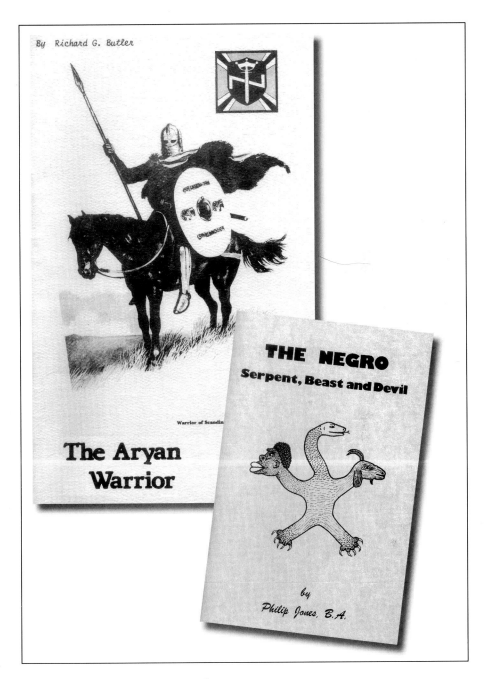

Pamphlet cover art from the Far Right.

ARYAN NATIONS

WE BELIEVE in the preservation of our Race, individually and collectively, as a people as demanded and directed by Yahweh. We believe our Racial Nation has a right and is under obligation to preserve itself and its members.

WE BELIEVE that the Cananite Jew is the natural enemy of our Aryan (White) Race. This is attested by scripture and all secular history. The Jew is like a destroying virus that attacks our racial body to destroy our Aryan culture and the purity of our Race.

WE BELIEVE that there is a battle being fought this day between the children of darkness (today known as Jews) and the children of light (Yahweh, The Everliving God), the Aryan Race, the true Israel of the bible. Revelations 12:10-11

37

Independent White Racialists

YOUR SKIN IS YOUR UNIFORM

YOUR FLAG IS YOUR VOICE

The concept of Leaderless Resistance

This page is evidence that concerned White people don't *have* to be members of an organization to fight for our freedoms and for *White survival!*

Some of you may already be aware that there exists an all-out war on our People, our culture, our heritage, and our very existence.

The most important thing that you can do to ensure our survival is to *educate yourself!* All three major tv news stations, ABC, NBC, and CBS are owned and controlled by jews. Documenting the jewish influence on our media, banking, law, and economic institutions would fill thousands of Web pages!

The Web of Hate, a special publication of the Anti-Defamation League, documents an abundance of hate materials on the World Wide Web.

HAIL THE ORDER

□ What is THE ORDER?
□ The Bruder Schweigen's Declaration of War.
□ The last testament from Bob Matthews, father of the second American Revolution.
□ P.O.W. Richard Scutari answers the question: Was it worth it?
□ P.O.W. Gary Yarbrough writes about unity.
□ P.O.W. David Lane writes about the American Monstrosity.
□ An Appeal from David on his illegal and malicious imprisonment.
□ Some of David's religious teachings.

Great links:

Once you have gained the necessary knowledge essential to our survival, motivate yourself and **get active!** Lead by example, and take it upon yourself to do whatever you feel comfortable doing, as long as you are doing **something** for your race!

We must secure the existence of our people
and a future for White children

SPECIAL YEAR-END EDITION: 1994

KLANWATCH
INTELLIGENCE REPORT

A PROJECT OF THE SOUTHERN POVERTY LAW CENTER   MARCH 1995/#77

Aryan Nations Stages Alarming Comeback in 1994

Neo-Nazi Group Sweeps into 15 States with Aggressive Recruiting Campaign

■ Aryan Nations—once the most violent, radical neo-Nazi group in North America—exploded in 1994 with a burst of spectacular growth after years of decline.

The Idaho-based group swept into 15 new states last year after being in only three in 1993. Richard Butler, who founded the Hitler-worshipping organization two decades ago, boasted recently that Aryan Nations will be in 30 states by year's end.

The phenomenal growth of Aryan Nations was the most startling development in the white supremacist world in 1994—a year that saw much of the organized hate movement in the United States settle into stagnation and decline. During 1994, the nation's largest Klan group fractured, the number two Klan organization went out of business, the neo-Nazi Skinhead movement dwindled, and many white supremacists scattered to the anti-government militias springing up across the country. (See related story on page 9)

The recent frenzy of activity at Aryan Nations is reminiscent of the group's heyday in the early 1980s when Butler's militancy spawned a violent band of terrorists called The Order. The gang (continued on page 5)

Skinheads Charged in Family Murders

Two Skinhead Brothers Linked to Aryan Nations' Leader

■ Two Pennsylvania Skinhead brothers charged with the brutal murders of their parents and younger brother may have acted under the influence of Aryan Nations leader and Identity "minister" Mark Thomas. The teenage brothers frequented Identity meetings and other racist functions at Thomas' 24-acre compound near Macungie, Penn., just a few miles from their home. According to one former member of Thomas' group, the white supremacist often threatened some of his teenage followers'

Left to right: Bryan Freeman, David Freeman and Nelson Birdwell III.

parents, calling them "race traitors."

Bryan Freeman, 17, and his brother, David, 16, allegedly bludgeoned and stabbed to death their mother, father and 11-year-old brother in the family's home near Allentown, Penn., (continued on page 2)

Klanwatch report confirms resurgence of the Far Right.

Harrison, Arkansas

Harrison, Arkansas, is an all-white Ozark town eager to tart itself up for the free-spending tourists. A town, however, with the wine-dark stain of a lynching in its past, a scar all the chamber of commerce scrubbing cannot wash away. As a stranger, I sense this in the giggling conversations of the teenage waitresses in a cafe.

"Nigger girl says this to Ricky . . . "

I sense it in the hard-eyed looks of the long-haired factory workers drinking beer by the side of the road, their dusty, jacked-up trucks bunched together like lathered saddle horses in Dodge City. It's written on the wall of the men's room of the wilted Ozark Mall, where somebody scratched "I love Jesus" on the toilet paper dispenser and someone else wrote, "Hitler was right." A retired cop from Chicago reading a week-old copy of the Tribune tells me the natives are decent and honest, but "ya can't figure the sons of bitches out."

I'm in Harrison looking for Thom Robb, a racist who flaunts his credentials—Identity minister, National Chaplain of the Knights of the Ku Klux Klan, publisher of the *White Patriot* and *Torch* newsletters—like other folks showcase Ph.D.s. I caught a glimpse of him at a riotous KKK march in Washington, D.C., in the early eighties. I have since interviewed him for *Newsweek* magazine and followed his career. Robb was a regular speaker at Aryan Nations and dozens of other far-right rallies and convocations. At a 1988 forum in Lawrence, Kansas, he accused anti-Klan protesters of being "filled with hatred and bigotry." In January 1990 he was in Pulaski, Tennessee, birthplace of the KKK, at the head of a column of 250 Klansmen, skinheads and neo-Nazis in defiance of a court order.

A man at a filling station tells me I can find Robb's wife working at Mass Merchandisers on Highway 43. A few miles down the road, I come upon a warehouse looming like a monolith against the green mountains. I move past corporate checkpoints manned by security guards dressed in NASA-style jumpsuits, me all smiles and credentials. A thousand people labor like ants, filling catalog orders in a noisy, multi-tiered workspace the size of an aircraft carrier. Forklifts zoom by like Indy cars, their noise deafening.

I ask to see Muriel Robb.

Fifteen minutes later, a plain-looking woman dressed in a jumpsuit arrives. Fear and suspicion dance across her face.

"What does the stranger want?"

"Is he a federal agent?"

"A threat to my husband . . . my job?"

"How will I feed our three kids?"

I introduce myself, ask for directions to her house. Quickly, I wonder if she'll call her husband, let him know I'm here to talk to him.

Her head bobs as I'm talking. She agrees, eager to get me away from the staring eyes of her foreman and coworkers.

I first interviewed Thom Robb in the mid-eighties in Harrison. At his suggestion, we met at the Ramada Inn, where he said the luncheon buffet was unbeatable. I watched him circle the parking lot in a beat-up car, as if wary of being ambushed by some hate-filled Jewish Defense League thug—already a dead man if someone truly wanted to kill him. He got out, a short guy whose thinning hair was racing against a receding chin. In a rumpled, ill-fitting gray suit, Robb looked like a used-car salesmen having a rough quarter. He brought along a bodyguard—a tall, fierce-looking Klansman with eyebrows like hawk wings. It struck me that, physically, the blond Aryan with the KKK pin in his lapel was all the things Thom Robb wanted to be.

Dividing his attention between chocolate pudding and peach cobbler, Robb gave me the standard spiel about traitors in Washington "busing little children into niggertown," swarming aliens "who've never heard of George Washington," the miracle of Identity Christianity "which breaks the power Jewry has over America," Aryan superiority. "The nature of our people tends toward duty, kindness, love and sacrifice," he said, spooning more sugary dessert into his mouth.

"You know, it's ironic," he said, swallowing, "we're the enemies of all the liberals, communists and queers. At the same time, the conservatives, moralists, anti-abortionists and prayer-in-the-school crowd—which we agree with on most issues—despise us."

Only when he got to Jews did Robb drop the dispassionate guise, let the philosophical lamenting go, gave up trying to appear reasonable or clever. "*I hate Jews*," he snarled. I thought of my daughter living innocent and unknowing under his curse. I wanted to smash Thom Robb's rodent face.

"I hate race-mixing Jews," he ranted, as people at the other tables began turning our way. "I hate Jews that are destroying our country! I hate Jews that spit on our flag! I hate Jews that rob our sustenance to support the state of Israel! I don't hate them just because they are Jewish. They have this power!"

That was it. I had more than enough quotes for my *Newsweek* story. And Robb had cooperated nicely, saying the terrible things I had come to hear. Millions of readers would read those words. Over the years, I saw that vicious rant repeated in other newspapers and periodicals. In a very real sense, I'd birthed his rage, played midwife to his hatemongering, gave sorrow words.

Where, I now wondered, did it come from?

Thomas Arthur Robb was born in Detroit, the son of a builder and sometime insurance salesman. His mother, Elda, he says, worked as clerk in a store. The Robbs were a middle-class family, conservative, religious, hard-shell Baptists. "There were no economic problems," Robb insists. "And I wasn't beat up by Negroes when I was a kid."

It was his mother, "a strong patriot aware of the Jewish involvement in communism," who was his creator, whose life encompassed 50 years of far-right extremism, who breast-fed her son's alienation. Elda Robb left the simple verities of the Baptists for the charismatic preaching of Kenneth Goff, an early Identity preacher. Goff, in his turn, was a disciple of Gerald L. K. Smith, the pre-World War II fascist rabble-rouser who organized an antigovernment, antiunion, Red-baiting crusade with, research shows, the backing of powerful petroleum- and auto-industry magnates.

When attacking Franklin Roosevelt and the New Deal didn't energize a populace hoping to escape the Depression, Smith, whose popularity, if not his positions, parallels Rush Limbaugh's today, turned to outright hatemongering. In the 1930s and 1940s, Smith earned his sobriquet, the "Dean of American Anti-Semitism," inciting riot and mayhem against the ragged immigrants and refugees who escaped Hitler. *The Protocols of the Learned Elders of Zion* was his bible.

The *Protocols*, an enduring forgery created by White Russian anti-Semites, first cropped up in the United States in the early 1900s. The tract depicts the Jew not just as a religious and social outcast, but as history's Satanic conspirator. In the *Protocols* a Jewish "Elder" describes a plot against Christianity that has been under way for centuries. "The goyim are a flock of sheep and we are the wolves." A Zionist "hidden hand" manipulates the economies and political systems of the West, fomenting war and revolution, accumulating power, killing off hated Gentiles.

Jews control not only capitalism but communism and socialism as well. The press, trade unions and school systems are controlled by Zionists promoting the corrupt theories of Marx, Darwin and Nietzsche. Oblivious Christians are mocked as "alcoholized animals bemused with drink." The *Protocols'* bigotry spread far beyond the fringe. In 1920, Henry Ford, a virulent anti-Semite, commissioned a series of articles, "The International Jew: The World's Problem," that ran in the *Dearborn Independent* newspaper for nearly two years.

Gerald Smith, who had drawn hundreds of thousands of pro-fascist fundamentalists to his Depression-era rallies, ran for president in 1944, promising, among other things, to investigate whether "the New Deal was heavily-staffed by a certain type of Jewish bureaucrat." In 1946, he reprinted the *Dearborn Independent's* anti-Semitic articles. Smith's newsletter, *The Cross and the Flag*, began calling for the deportation of all blacks. Elda Robb agreed completely.

These were the storybooks and heroes upon which young Thomas Robb was raised. One of his early memories: sitting in the living room with his mother, illumined by the pale light of the black and white TV.

"We're watching Jack Parr fawning over Fidel Castro."

"Mom, who is this Castro?"

Elda, squinting at the screen, stares at the bearded Cuban, face puckered as if she'd bitten a lemon.

"Hey!" she shrieks. "This guy's a Communist!"

The family moved to Tucson, and Robb matured into one of those nondescript kids haunting the halls of every American high school. Overlooked, ignored, naked in his neediness, thirsting for attention. Alone in his room he stared at his mirrored reflection, dreaming of becoming a lawyer, a politician, *somebody*. Reality shattered the mirror. "I was just the average John Doe," he says. "Mostly goofing off."

If the misspellings and grammatical manglings in his newsletters are any indication, Robb didn't absorb much education. Eager to please his mama, he joined the John Birch Society, practically a mainstream organization in Goldwater's Arizona. Robb liked the hidden messages in Goldwater's rhetoric, the willingness to let the states decide issues like integration, the eagerness, Robb thought with a smile, "to keep the niggers in their place."

Like most teenagers, Robb was too self-involved to wrap himself completely in any cause. He says he was not particularly anti-Semitic at the time. Was not Jesus Christ a Jew? One day he came across a *Communism is Jewish* sticker on a wall.

"I ripped it down."

All that changed when he enrolled, at Elda's insistence, at Kenneth Goff's Soldiers of the Cross Bible Institute in Evergreen, Colorado. Robb, who met his wife, there, immersed himself in Identity teaching, emerging two years later a "minister" and fire-breathing racist. "I became," he says, laughing, "a born-again white man."

After Bible school, Robb returned to Tucson. One of his brothers had become a policeman, another was moving to California, where he'd found work as a building contractor. Like so many others he would meet, they began to distance themselves. Didn't matter. Robb, trained as a printer, began publishing his first hate sheet, *The Message of Old Monthly*, in Arizona, about the same time that Ty Hardin, the old television cowboy, was trying to organize a primitive, heavily armed militia he called the Arizona Patriots.

Robb's newsletter evolved into the *Torch* and, later, into the KKK's *White Patriot*—skinny, half-literate tabloids trying to appear thick with readership and meaning, all trumpeting the same racist message.

His family—Elda, of course, defended him—now began furiously backpedaling, furthering Robb's sense of being a prophet scorned by his kindred. "They're traditional Baptists and they are against race-mixing," he says bitterly. "But to them *racist* is one of the bad words. . . . And I've become one."

He had trouble making a living, almost a given on the fringe. He had no choice; this was his calling, no different from the lives of the apostles. "I could blend into society," Robb insists. "I could go along and do the big act. But I sacrifice so my children and even the children of those who are against me can have a future. Thousands of white people probably hate me. Yet I'm willing to suffer for them."

Adolescent dreams forgotten, Robb moved to Missouri,

where he got on with a poultry operation. The sagging, odiferous chicken houses in the rural South are hard places to imagine oneself as either an Aryan warrior or Arthurian knight, but easy places to imagine plots hatched by international conspirators. When the poultry operations began to employ Vietnamese and Chicano workers, Robb, unhappy with the stench, moved to Arkansas to labor in a factory, forced, he says, "to continue my quote, unquote *hate* on the side."

Years pass, and I meet Robb at the same luncheon buffet at the Ramada Inn in Harrison. This time he helps himself to fried chicken and macaroni salad. He's dressed in a nice blue suit, wearing aviator sunglasses and modish sideburns. It's like he's gone from selling Chevy's to Amway. His hair is thinner, his paunch thicker, but, as appearances go, he's on the upswing. Instead of the Nazi bodyguard with the hawk-wing eyebrows, he's brought an attractive young woman with him. She turns out to be his daughter Rachel.

And he's carrying a dog-eared copy of *The Autobiography of Malcolm X* under his arm.

"What is that about?" I'm thinking.

The last time we spoke, Robb said he wouldn't even "tolerate" any blacks in the United States. He's mellowed, willing to work with black separatists. "Negroes are not human the way white people are human," he says, chewing on a mouthful of chicken. "But I've got this great tape of Farrakhan calling the Jewish religion a gutter religion. The guy's tremendous! First time I heard it, I'm sitting there going 'Good for you! Right on!'

"Now, I'm reading Malcolm X's autobiography. I identify with his struggle." He pauses, then adds with a wink, "If the Negroes think they're the Chosen People and we're animals who ran around the caves of Europe, let 'em."

Rachel is daddy's girl, Robb's pride and joy, tied to him by the same umbilical cord that kept him bound to his racist mother. She is Robb's proof that the patriot movement is not composed of losers and misfits. She's popular, a cheerleader, good-looking enough, Thom says, to place in Arkansas beauty contests. He wants her to study hard and become a doctor, hide her racism ("Why blow an opportunity to pull down $100,000 a year?") until she's assimilated into the mainstream.

"Tell him you're the editor of the high school paper," Robb says.

"Somebody else is doing that now."

"And the Beta Club."

"I'm in the Future Homemakers of America."

"You see," says Robb, "we're average American people."

He's right. Rachel seems more interested in getting her own car and winning back a wandering boyfriend than strutting for her father.

"Tell him why you're in the Ku Klux Klan," Robb says, a little frustrated.

"Rea-lly. It's not a big deal at school."

He looks at her sourly, then tries another tack. "The government has driven a wedge into the white family," he says. "Look in the papers, 'Homosexuals, women and other minorities. . . .' Women are *not* a minority. The white *man* is the natural ruler of the family. Our enemies are trying to develop a conflict between the man and *his* wife and children. Imagine this: My daughter can't take an aspirin in school without a permission slip, but she can go out and have an abortion without telling me!"

Rachel squirms uneasily, glances at her watch.

Robb, already galloping on to another subject, ignores her. Over the years, he has been careful about inciting violence. He's a leader, weak-chinned or not, a Bible-thumping minister who wouldn't do well in the homosexual hell holes, Aryan or otherwise, that are our prisons. But with the militias looming, with paranoid, antigovernment rhetoric leeching into the hearts and minds of Timothy McVeigh, Randy Weaver, militia leaders, and a thousand other dangerous and alienated men, he goes further.

"Throughout history, when society became corrupt, there was always a frontier we could retreat to. Now there's no retreat. We must take a stand. Asking me if I'm for violence is foolish. It'd be like going to George Washington in 1776 and saying, 'Well, George, are you for violence?' Washington took up the gun to defend his home. If the colonists had lost, we'd be reading history books about the traitors Washington, Jefferson and Madison.

"If the war we're engaged in brings us victory," Robb says, dropping his napkin and heading for the dessert bar, "we'll be heroes."

On the way back, he stands over me, looks closely. "You're an I-talian right?"

"Yeah?"

"You were probably raised in an I-talian neighborhood."

"Yeah, South Brooklyn."

"How would you feel, if instead of the old faces, there were Asians running the stores?"

"There are some Puerto Ricans, a few Orthodox Jews running a knitting factory. . . ."

"Well?"

"I don't give a shit." I nod at Rachel. "Scuse my language."

She giggles. Robb glares.

I do love my old neighborhood, can't help but think of it during this interview. In fact, it hasn't changed all that much. The Gowanus Canal is less polluted, but Carmela Persico and the other old ladies still sit on the stoops outside their houses gossiping; the wise guys are on the corner of Carroll Street and Third Avenue, scratching their balls and trying to handicap horses off the racing forms. You can smell tomato sauce cooking and meatballs frying on Sunday mornings. But too many of my friends, my cousins, my kid brother Thomas, are lying dead in Greenwood Cemetery, killed by crime, drug abuse, HIV infection. The organized crime guys, the big shots I thought were cool, are behind the death and corruption. Robb is right; there are *mud people* destroying our nation, but the term has nothing to do with skin color or ethnic origin.

I turn my attention to pretty Rachel. She tells me she wants to write stories. She would like to be a journalist. "That's a problem," I say, "being in the Klan and all." Nope, no way would she give up her racism for career success. "If people get uptight because I'm in the Klan, that's their problem. Jews run the country, and it doesn't look like it's in very good shape."

Thom Robb, about to make another pass at the dessert bar before the waiters remove the buffet, stands beaming at her.

He walks away. I smile, then ask her point blank, "You think your father's a nut, don't you? Tell the truth?"

"There's a need for it, definitely," she says. "There are mongrels at school. *Mongrels* who want white girlfriends. There needs to be somebody like my Dad making sure that doesn't happen."

"Right," I mutter, as if I understand.

Mongrels, I'm thinking, as Robb rejoins us, eager to get on with his interview. Such an ugly word coming from such a pretty girl.

Christianity is a 24-hour-a-day, seven-day-a-week experience. We're here to live that life.

Robert Millar, Elohim City

Chapter 8

Elohim City and Oklahoma City

In Mountain Home, Arkansas, an old Nazi calling himself Kurt Saxon tells me about a survivalist commune, Elohim (God's) City, hidden in the mountains near the Oklahoma border. The last such place I'd visited, the Covenant, the Sword, the Arm of the Lord (CSA), I'd been run off by bearded cretins waving automatic rifles. Later, I learned CSA's "Christians" had stockpiled enough cyanide to poison a small city. In the 1980s, Saxon had given up his goose-stepping for a more lucrative occupation—gun trading and producing do-it-yourself manuals on how to make bombs and other weapons. His biggest seller: *The Poor Man's James Bond.*

In the late 1940s, I'm told, Elohim City's patriarch, Robert Millar, a Mennonite, felt the hand of God upon him. His arms flew up. He was moved to dance, sing and shout his joy. Elohim, or Yahweh, revealed many secrets to Reverend Millar. Among them: Jesus was Aryan. This blond Messiah would soon return to redeem a small remnant of the white race. Upon that rock Millar built his church, first a campsite in Maryland, now a colony lost in the fog of the Ozarks. Millar's son says the old man travels the country constantly, searching for those called to a "deeper walk."

One of them, the cop-killer Wayne Snell; another, the alleged Oklahoma City bomber, Timothy McVeigh.

On a hot autumn afternoon, I drive west toward Fayetteville, Arkansas, to find Millar's commune. Highway 62 near Beaver Lake is a ribbon of curves and switchbacks that reduce visibility to 100-foot sections of blistered asphalt. A colossal statue looms unexpectedly before me, soaring above the treetops. This, I learn, is the Christ of the Ozarks, a seven-story limestone Messiah blessing the souvenir shops, Christmas stores and fudge parlors of Eureka Springs, a 19th-century spa once known for its fieldstone hotels, mud baths and mineral waters.

Christ of the Ozarks, Eureka Springs' Bible Museum and its Christ-Only Art Gallery are the sacred projects of Gerald L. K. Smith, who was Elda Robb's inspirational preacher. Smith died, happily, before he could complete his Arkansas masterwork, a life-sized replica of the Holy Land. Somebody else built another tourist attraction, a theme park called Dog Patch, recreating the old Al Capp cartoon.

Smith lies buried, another mockery, at the foot of his monumental statue.

To reach Elohim City, one must pass through purgatory.

Oklahoma's slumping oil industry, years of drought and agricultural distress have all taken their toll. Many of its small towns are lifeless or decaying, the faces of working people eroded by despair. Even the children seem listless and dispirited.

I catch glimpses of young men, long-haired and sullen in raggedy denim, crippled by divorce and schools that failed them, driving rusting hot rods or chopped motorcycles throbbing with menace. Drinking, smoking, snorting Mexican dope, getting smashed on animal tranquilizers, waiting—many of them, I imagine—to commit the senseless crime that will lock them away. An immutable cycle, regular as the seasons. Among them move Native Americans with braided hair, remnants of the Cherokee Nation. The Trail of Tears ended here, a fitting place, without light or hope.

One roadside sign reads "Warning: Hitchhikers May Be Escaping Prisoners."

Adair County is one of Oklahoma's poorest; Stillwell its county seat. On a Friday, I walk into the basement office of Sheriff Russell Neff, a man with the lined, leathery face and sinewy arms of a sodbuster. I introduce myself, ask for directions to Oak Ridge Mountain, atop which Elohim City is built.

In rural America, sheriffs are kings of their counties, with comfortable offices, secretaries and deputies. Walls are heavy with awards, photos and plaques, the Man grinning right there alongside politicians and business leaders, thinking about next year's reelection. Usually there's a display case for schoolkids and matrons to gawk at, filled with hash pipes and confiscated marijuana cigarettes, guns and rusty knives, occasionally some local item or artifact: gold nuggets, Indian jewelry or carvings.

Neff has nothing. Just a crowded desk and some cardboard cartons piled on top of file cabinets in a dingy room. This sheriff looks like a man who has held his finger in the dike way too long. The weekend hasn't even begun yet, and he's having a bad time. A prisoner escaped from the county courthouse during trial this morning.

"I don't give a good Goddamn . . . ," Neff snarls into his phone. "Find him!"

He hangs up, rubs his temple like he's got a bad headache, then warns me off the commune: "Had trouble enough already with them people. Don't need no more."

At that moment, a woman walks into the office trailing a brood of tattered kids. She looks right through me.

"He's drunk again," she says. "Been beating on me, smashing things."

Neff stares at her in silence.

There are no tears, no sobbing. Her speech is toneless, hopeless, but everything is confirmed in the children's faces. One son is about 14, dressed in a tee-shirt, hair close-cropped, standing there, fists clenched beside his momma, knowing he's no match for his old man. Not yet, anyway.

"Will you find him and stop him?" the woman pleads. "Serve them papers?"

Neff lifts himself wearily from his desk. He will go.

Over his shoulder, he tosses me directions, a jumble of twists and turns that will take me to the top of the mountain. That afternoon I get lost, find myself back in Arkansas, where I stop at a roadside store almost empty of merchandise. A fat lady is watching a soap opera on a blurry TV, its reception provided by an old rabbit-ear antenna; the woman grudgingly gets up to sell me a Milky Way. I ask directions; she shrugs her ignorance. Down the road I pull up at a beggarly garage sale; another woman sits in the October sun hoping to sell a used pair of men's shoes and some faded blouses. I ask for a phone to call Neff. She takes me into her house, points to the phone and goes back outside, innocent and trusting, another side of Oklahoma. I want to buy something to repay her kindness. There's nothing.

Elohim City sits above this vale of tears on a dirt road strewn with boulders and fallen trees, five miles past the last recognizable landmark, its temple an ovoid blister erupted on the mountain's flank. Imagine Stephen King's take on a sixties-geodesic dome. A crooked archway is cut into the polyurethane and fiberglass structure, which rests on a low fieldstone foundation. The dome is lumpy and misshapen, one end dimpled, like a baby's head squeezed by a forceps. A circular window, maybe the top of an old glass coffee table, fills the depression.

A dozen children in shorts and tee-shirts are playing in the road. A few approach me shyly, others giggle; two older ones run off to find a grown-up. I stand there smiling awkwardly, as a burly motorcyclist wearing a World War II army helmet rumbles across a stubbled field to check me out. He promptly falls off the bike.

Tho' I sometimes fear this place and find it hard to fill,
I could never live outside the center of Your Will.

—A plaque on the wall of Elohim City

On April 5, 1995, two weeks before the bombing of the Murrah
building in Oklahoma City, Timothy McVeigh made a phone
call to Elohim City, trying perhaps to reach Robert Millar.
Eighteen months earlier, McVeigh was stopped by police for a
traffic violation on Route 220, just a few miles from the compound.

Millar insists he does not know McVeigh and that the accused
bomber never visited Elohim City; but there are disturbing links
between McVeigh and Millar's white separatists. Law-enforcement officials now believe the Oklahoma City bombing was pre-
cisely tied to the execution of Richard Wayne Snell.

Snell, another bearded "end time" fanatic haunting the
Ozarks, had murdered a black Arkansas trooper, Louis Bryant, in
1984. He'd executed pawnshop owner Wayne Stumpp during a
robbery, mistakenly believing the man was Jewish. A member of
the CSA commune, Snell had planned or participated in a
number of other terror bombings. Cornered by police, after the
Bryant killing, he was shot seven times in a furious gun battle.
He survived to face execution 12 years later by the authorities
he'd waged war upon.

Perhaps McVeigh wanted to pay homage to a fellow Aryan
warrior. More troubling: at a hearing one supporter warned
Arkansas clemency board members the "wrath of God" would
descend if Snell were put to death.

Did Snell know McVeigh's murderous intent?

His last words before his execution were, "Look over your
shoulder, justice is coming." The bombing had actually taken
place 12 hours before, but he wouldn't have known the timing,
isolated on Death Row.

Robert Millar was Snell's spiritual adviser. Among the fringe groups it was widely known that Millar would lay claim to the body of the killer—now a martyr in the jihad against ZOG—and bury it in Elohim City's sacred ground.

A decade earlier, Millar had played pastor to the ranting CSA founder Jim Ellison. A polygamous, vest-pocket Hitler, Ellison slept with a stolen U.S. Army LAW anti-tank missile next to his bed. A former Baptist preacher, he had discovered the peculiar joys of Identity Christianity: he took four wives and ordered other men to sleep in dormitories. One of his warriors abandoned CSA, complaining that Ellison "had been plowing with my heifer."

CSA survived by collecting welfare checks and stripping wrecked cars. Its children begged in the streets of nearby towns. Even other extremists referred to the place as "the Jonestown of the Ozarks." Overrun by 300 FBI, ATF and Arkansas law-enforcement agents in April 1985, the compound contained a workshop for converting semi-automatic rifles to machine guns, caches of stolen military plastic explosives, a half-built armored car and a drum of cyanide.

Ellison was convicted on weapons violations and federal conspiracy charges involving the bombings of a church in Springfield, Missouri, a Jewish community center in Bloomington, Indiana, and a gas pipeline in Missouri, targeted, according to one of the conspirators, "to spread chaos."

When I arrive, there are 50 people inhabiting Elohim City, half of them apparently related to the Millars. They live in wood-frame houses and beat-up trailers clustered around the temple. Despite their avowed desire to "keep out of the system," a number are collecting food stamps. The camp has electricity, running water, even a few TV antennas. Residents observe strict dietary laws—they believe themselves Israelites—and study Hebrew. The men drink an occasional beer, the women wear lipstick and modern clothes. The Sabbath and other holy days are determined by Hebrew astrological calculations.

I'm standing, surrounded by children, when Robert Millar's sons John and Fred stride up to me. Fred is wary, suspicious. He gives a false name but later forgets it. John, older, is soft-spoken, quite handsome, more forthcoming. He's willing to talk to me but only about religion. We walk over to a pile of logs and sit down. Nearby, a group of men are fiddling with a rusted V-8 engine used to power a dilapidated sawmill.

The engine coughs, spits, dies. The men fiddle with the carburetor.

Millar describes Elohim City as a kind of family-oriented monastery. "It's proper for a people to minister unto the deity," he says. "Christianity is a 24-hour-a-day, seven-day-a-week experience. We're here to live that life."

Unable to get the motor running for more than a few seconds, the men drift back toward the temple. They banter back and forth with John Millar. In a month, it'll be cold; there's wood to cut, homes to insulate, the endless, repetitive drudgery of rural living. The rewards, Millar insists, far outnumber any sacrifices. "We're the happiest people there are. We sing, we dance. We have fun. I have a relationship with my children that I cherish. I'm at home. I work with my sons. My daughters are with their mother. Where could I find that?"

In the blistered temple, under the flag with the Lion of Judah rampant, Millar's children perform ritual dances and chant the praises of Yahweh. I, an outsider, am to understand these celebrations are fun. "Jesus said, 'I come that you may have life and have it more abundantly,'" Millar tells me. "In modern terms that means, 'Live it up, have a good life!'"

Who can deny that? Millar is open and friendly as long as we talk about the joys of country living. He won't talk about Richard Snell and Jim Ellison and the lie their hatred gives to everything he says.

After awhile, we are joined by Ralph Hansen, the burly security chief who fell off his motorcycle as I walked up. Hansen says he gave up a booming contracting business in

Arizona to move to the Ozarks.

"The peace impressed me," he says.

Again I think of Wayne Snell. I mention him and Ellison to Millar. In the eighties, the machine-gun-toting killer was a familiar figure at Elohim City. Sometimes alone, sometimes with his wife and seven children, he camped and mingled with the congregation. Millar—a character witness at Snell's murder trials—tells me Snell was a "new Christian trying to find his way back to the face of God."

"Excuse me?"

Then he says Ellison, a man who dreamed of slaughtering his neighbors with cyanide and anti-tank rockets, who conspired to bomb churches and synagogues, is "a God-fearing man with a pastor's heart."

I pull a copy of Ellison's CSA *Journal* from my briefcase. I show it to the two men.

"Mr. Millar, you mind if I read you something?"

"If you want."

"Ellison wrote this. Just listen. 'There will be riots in the cities, famine and war. Parents will eat their children. Communists will kill white Christians and mutilate them. . . . Homosexuals will sodomize whoever they can. All but the elect will have the mark of the beast. . . .' It goes on and on."

They look at me. I might as well be speaking Chinese.

"You really think this guy is normal?" I say. "A pastor?"

"Why must you people always focus on the negative?" John Millar asks with some exasperation. Yahweh had given his father "signs." "We've had confirmation we're on the right track," he says, as if speaking to a child. "We might have some big changes to offer the world in the next few years."

I say nothing.

In 1995, when Timothy McVeigh began his long march to Oklahoma City and Snell had finally begun hearing the last strains of the executioner's song, James Ellison was believed to be back at Elohim City, girding for war.

If I sat down and thought about it, I could have killed both troopers.

—David Tate, Aryan Nations

Chapter 9

The Cop Killer

Jefferson City, Missouri

The penitentiary squats in the heart of Jefferson City, its limestone walls leaking rage and fear. The Wall, as locals call it, was built at a time when fortresses kept savagery outside the gates. Now the barbarians are locked inside. The prison is thick with murderers, molesters, rapists, punks and snitches serving lengthy sentences, deviant life forms devolved beyond even the pretense of rehabilitation.

"We can't shoot them," one guard tells me as I stand around

waiting for my interview. "All we can hope for is that they kill each other."

The prison yard is barren and dust-blown, salted with a hundred years of sweat and blood. Aryan musclemen, their naked torsos covered with swastikas and Nazi regalia, line one wall, flexing, posing, absentmindedly stroking themselves. Across from them, mirror images carved in obsidian, are the blacks, many wearing loose-fitting dashikis, bracelets, do-rags on their heads. Chicanos, draped in baggy chinos, denim shirts, tattooed with *santos* (saints) and *placas* (gang emblems) celebrating *la Raza* (the Race). And Indians, black hair flowing to their waists.

A dozen boom boxes blare rap music, metallica, and redneck country songs. Transvestites in scarves and tight red skirts skitter across the yard giggling, talking way too loud. Everyone stares, everyone seems stoned, drowsy rattlesnakes basking in the sun.

"Stay close," a guard tells me as I pass through a series of gates and steel doors as complex as an air lock.

"The warden doesn't want to get you killed." His buddies grin.

"Right," I say.

We descend into the bowels of the place, down narrow, windowless corridors, green paint peeling from the walls. The smells are overpowering: disinfectant, greasy food, sweat, fear, incense, cheap cologne.

"Yo, punk!"

The guard next to me seems oblivious to this threat, so I try to ignore the skinny blond guy lounging against the wall.

"Yeah, you, big man. You mine, mother." His Okie twang jars and jangles the street jive.

"You're maahn."

I'm sweating by the time we approach a small steel room on Level One. "David Tate is the most dangerous man in here," one of the guards brags. He's not laughing.

Tate, an Identity Christian, had machine-gunned to death a Missouri state trooper named Jimmie Linegar on Highway 86. Linegar was also a Christian; his misfortune was to flag down Tate's van on a routine traffic check.

A few months earlier in Idaho, Tate's father, a dairy farmer dressed in bib overalls, asked me to visit David when I got to Missouri. Soft-spoken, painfully polite, Charles Tate stood tamping tobacco into his pipe while we spoke.

"David is as fine a son as anyone could have," he tells me. "When his younger sisters wanted to go skating or to a movie, David always took them. It was as good as if we parents were there. . . ."

I notice two framed photographs on the wall behind Charles Tate. One is a shot of three muscle-bound prisoners, all big as Hulk Hogan and covered with swastikas. They're posing with a portrait of Adolf Hitler. Next to it is a photo of a lardy teenager with soft, sensuous features. He's wearing a Nazi SS uniform.

I imagine this kid jerking off as he drowns kittens.

"Is that . . . David?" I ask.

"Oh no," Tate mumbles. "Just one of our friends." We talk for a few more minutes. I watch his thick, ink-covered hands as he polishes his eyeglasses over and over again with a hand-kerchief.

"You will go see David?"

"I'd like to."

David Tate is remembered as a quiet kid, not particularly interested in school, books or sports. He will later describe his life to me as "about average." He took a few skiing lessons, more as a way to meet girls than for the sport. When his father and mother, Betty, joined Richard Butler's Aryan Nations, David, barely out of his teens, went along. Butler put him in charge of the printing press. Later he silk-screened neo-Nazi tee-shirts.

In Hayden Lake, Idaho, he met Robert Matthews, Frank

Silva, Gary Yarbrough and other Order members, men who were about to launch their war on society. They seemed strong and brave. Twenty-year-old Tate, short and shy, basked in the attention Matthews showered on him. When he joined, Matthews called him "Doc," a secret code name.

Tate wasn't like the others. When he watched as Walter West, a suspected informant, was dragged into the woods, bludgeoned with a hammer and shot, Tate puked all over himself. West's murder became a joke in The Order, something laughed about in bars. His killers toasted each other, singing the Beatles' "Maxwell's Silver Hammer."

By the spring of 1985, Matthews was dead. The war against ZOG was not going well. Surviving Order members were cooperating with the feds, in jail or on the run.

Without Matthews, Tate says he felt "like a branch cut off from the trunk of a tree." He was scared, but he tried not to panic. "I'm a warrior on a sacred quest," he told himself. His parents, Pastor Butler, generations of unborn white children, were counting on him. . . .

Tate drove his 1975 Chevrolet van, bearing Nevada plates, cross-country into Arkansas. He'd hoped to find refuge at the CSA compound on Bull Shoals Lake. On April 15, he pulled out of a campground near Rogers, Arkansas, heading north toward Branson, Missouri.

Hidden beneath a false floor in the van were five machine guns, 35 hand grenades, dynamite and a whiskey bottle filled with nitroglycerine, enough firepower to put Tate in prison for 20 years. He was carrying stores of survival equipment, packs, sleeping bags, fake ID cards, police scanners, ski masks.

After trooper Linegar and his partner, Allen Hines, pulled Tate over, a dispatcher radioed back information that the Oregon driver's license registered to "Matthew Mark Samuels" was a fake. Linegar, an experienced officer, didn't take the warning seriously enough. Perhaps he thought the scruffy, baby-faced kid wearing jeans and a print shirt was a car thief or small-time drug smuggler. He never suspected one of God's dragons lay seething.

Tate's hands closed on the short, brutal weapon beside him, a silencer-equipped machine gun. Linegar approached the driver's door, Hines edged along the passenger side. Tate kicked open the door. A twitch of the trigger and Linegar was spinning backward, hit six times. His bulletproof vest stopped five of the slugs, the sixth caught him unprotected under the arm and pierced his thorax. In the same instant, Tate whirled and shot Hines three times, then abandoned the van and fled into the forest. Hines radioed for help too late. Linegar bled to death on the pavement.

Five days later, hounded by hundreds of law-enforcement agents and National Guardsmen, Tate was arrested hiding in a park in Forsyth, Missouri.

I'm studying the graffiti in the prison's tiny visiting room when a young man emerges, slim and delicate. He's handcuffed, dressed in a coarse gray jumpsuit, his face and neck covered with red welts—a reaction, he says, to the hay-fever medicine he's been taking. Tate has been brought up from solitary confinement, a ten-by-twelve cell deep under the ground, a place he says is swarming with roaches.

The Wall will circumscribe his life for the next 60 years, barring revolution or an act of clemency by the Missouri governor. He doesn't understand this yet. With his parted sandy hair and neatly trimmed mustache, Tate looks like a management trainee in an insurance agency. He has an ironic, self-deprecating laugh. A laugh that will be lost on the brutal leering men upstairs.

He doesn't know this yet, either. Or what lies ahead. He tells me he reads his Bible and clings to Identity Christianity. He thinks he is bearing the white man's burden, just as his father told me back in Idaho. "God says in His book that we will go through different tribulations and hard times," he tells me. "God chose the position I'm in."

In the next breath, he's excited that this prison has a TV and basketball and handball courts. "A visiting room with lots of seats. You can get lunch and pop and candy bars. That kind of stuff." He laughs his strange laugh. "It's hotel lobbyish."

A month before, Tate was allowed his first walk around the yard. Within minutes, he had the attention of the black gangsters. They encircled him, and a "white boy" slipped a homemade shiv into his hand. Scared shitless, he was holding the knife in front of him when the guards beat him to the ground and threw him back in solitary.

He's locked in his cell 23 hours a day, with an hour to eat, shower and exercise in a narrow dog run. He has begun preaching to other inmates through the walls and vents of his cell. Sometimes he's able to slip reading materials under their cell doors. He tells me, "I'm opening a lot of new minds," then laughs at the absurdity of this.

Is he scared? "The blacks that understand my religion understand racial separation," he tells me. "I don't believe in destroying any race." He pauses, then adds, "I'm not into the things that get you into trouble, drugs and homosexuality."

He's not into these things. A slender, fair-haired boy who wants to read the Bible and convert his brethren, who has killed a cop . . . who is locked behind the Wall. He says he's got a girlfriend; she "read about me and comes to visit." Maybe they'll be getting married. When he's lonely, Tate says he escapes by reading books about "knights and armor and that kind of thing."

The handcuffs are real, and they are cutting into David's thin wrists. The Wall is real. He tells me he regrets killing 33-year-old Linegar, a married man with a five-year-old daughter and a three-year-old son. "I was panicking," he says. "If I sat down and thought about it, I could have killed both troopers. I didn't know what to do. Being caught out in the woods shows you how prepared I was."

It's an odd lament, a glimpse, perhaps, of the mind behind that neat preppie appearance. A guard signals we have five minutes to finish the interview. I stare at Tate.

"Why did you get involved with this stuff?" I finally ask. "Look where it got you. . . . Look at your life!"

The cop-killer winces.

"I was a spark," he says, the friendliness gone. "We have all this filth and garbage in this country. I had to do something."

"What did you do, kill a cop? Linegar was married, you know. He had kids!"

"I felt I had a purpose," he says coldly. "I don't really feel what I did was wrong."

The guard comes into the room, hustles Tate away. The prisoner turns to me as I'm gathering my notebooks and tape recorder.

"I have a purpose still."

I think about this as I drive out from under the shadow of the prison. Outside town, Highway 54 is alive with autumn color. I think about the blessing David's parents bestowed on him and the bitter fruit it bore.

A week later, I call Charles Tate in Idaho. I tell him David is in good spirits. I hear him sigh. I imagine him polishing his glasses. "I haven't lost my son," he says after a long moment. "I've gained a son. His mission is not over. I brought him into it, but David understands better than I do."

Zionists paint a lot of their own swastikas and tip over their own tombstones. They like being victims.

—John Harrell, Christian Patriots Defense
League

Chapter 10

Extreme Unction
John Harrell and Brigadier General Jack Mohr

Licking, Missouri

Leaving David Tate locked away in his dungeon, I arrive at the Christian Patriots Defense League's 223-acre camp on a bright autumn afternoon, the sounds of hammers and power saws a welcome counterpoint to the dead air of the prison. Having researched the organization's newsletters, which endlessly urge white Christians to prepare themselves for Armageddon, I'm expecting another load of paramilitary horseshit. Instead, an apple-cheeked old man in a tee-shirt, sporting a shock of white hair, comes out to greet me. He pumps my hand like I'm his lost long brother, or maybe a customer in a used-car lot. It's John Harrell, who founded his far-right militia, the Christian Patriots Defense League (CPDL), back in 1977.

"Call me Johnny Bob!"

Over the years, Johnny Bob Harrell had spun off a half dozen other ominous-sounding organizations—the Citizens Emergency Defense System, the Save America Gun Club, the Paul Revere Club, the Women's Survival Corps, among them—at one point claiming some 25,000 members. A wild exaggeration, no doubt—since this particular camp seemed abandoned—but, as I'm discovering, these are more than paper organizations.

Harrell, like Butler, Robb, Peters and other extremist "leaders," was a node in the network, a well-spring of insinuation, propaganda and paranoia feeding the anger of those who felt displaced, abandoned or betrayed by the federal government. A man whose ideas leeched into the malleable minds of thousands and were clearly able to energize the violent few.

In the 1980s, Harrell hosted "Freedom Festivals" on his land—giddy, far-right Woodstocks that, over the years, drew thousands of so-called kinsmen who took part in knife-fighting, hand-to-hand combat, and training in homemade explosives, weapons and survival techniques. Visiting emissaries from Aryan Nations, the KKK and Identity Churches spewed antigovernment lectures and doomsday propaganda. Harrell's festivals were the places where networking and bonding occurred, where the isolated and the unholy presumably found each other.

The CPDL compound I visited lay close to the Missouri-Arkansas border, where the Elohim City and CSA communes were located; close to where Posse Comitatus hero Gordon Kahl was killed in his farmhouse bunker, to where David Tate and Wayne Snell murdered state troopers in cold blood, to where Thom Robb did his preaching.

"You Italian?" Harrell says, mispronouncing my name.
"Yeah."
"So, can you sing?"

He's bursting with energy and what must be folksy humor, like Garrison Keillor gone fascist. "I'm 70, I guess," he tells me. "Snow on the roof, but fire in the furnace yet." An all-American entrepreneur who made a fortune in construction and prefabricated mausoleums and built his dream house out there on the Illinois prairie: a replica of George Washington's Mount Vernon home, only bigger.

"I've got to make a few phone calls," he says. "Be right back and we'll talk. Yessir!"

For 35 years, he portrayed himself as a modern-day Paul Revere, sounding the alarm against society's collapse. He was God's own drill sergeant, rallying a segment of the white race to prepare for survival. Harrell was persistent. His newsletters kept coming years after I got my name on his mailing lists; I even got phone calls from Citizens Emergency Defense System's "military coordinators" in my area. The letters and "intelligence reports" put out by his "National Defense Coordinator," a tired old John Bircher calling himself "Brigadier General" Jack Mohr, were always the same:

> . . . Hispanic aliens with large sums of money are moving up the banks of the Mississippi. . . . Tanks with Russian insignia have been spotted 150 miles inside the Texas border. . . . Half the boat people arriving in the United States are Viet Cong pledged to carry the fight to our shores. . . . 15 men were picked up near El Paso carrying components for a nuclear device. . . .

"Mindless shit," I'm thinking, remembering the stuff and thinking about the unimportance of the sweaty old man I'd come all this way to see. But someone—Robert Matthews and David Tate in the 1980s, Timothy McVeigh and the 82nd Airborne Division skinheads who slaughtered a black couple in Fayetteville, North Carolina in 1995—was always out there listening, breathing, waiting, wanting to be part of something big and important, wanting to strike a blow.

"I was in the Mayo clinic dying of cancer."

"Excuse me?"

Johnny Bob is back and wants to tell me his life story.

"Go on," I say, taking a seat under a covered picnic table. I've no choice. I'm a thousand miles from nowhere.

"I had tumors all over me. Lymphatic cancers. Today they can stave 'em off some, but in the fifties, you'd be dead within a year. *Then it happened* on the night of June 16, 1959. It was like I was in a celestial blow torch. My flesh was singed but not disintegrated. The experience kept happening. I'd wake up in the night with an awesome presence in my room. I couldn't breathe. I'd throw my hands up on my face. It got so tiresome I thought, 'Gee I can't rest. . . .'"

"I bet," I mumble. He rolls right over me.

"Finally, I began to inquire of the Lord. I'm a Methodist by background, and I went to a Catholic college in Illinois for two years. My mother ran the state tax department there. . . . Anyway, I asked the Lord, 'What is this about?'

"He said, *'The nation is going through a crisis. I'll heal you if you warn the people of what is to come.'*

"I had four or five kids, enough money to never have to work again. I was 36 years old and dying. Gee whiz! What a time to leave!

"I said, 'I'll do what You want me to do.'"

God apparently wanted him to run for office in 1959 against U.S. senator Paul Douglas. Harrell ran an abrasive, rambunctious race ("I don't care if you vote for me or not. I ain't kissing your babies nor currying your favor."), attacking Douglas and the young liberal Democratic presidential candidate from Massachusetts, John Fitzgerald Kennedy.

"Of course, no one voted for me."

Harrell's campaign was based on his religious beliefs, a mixture of Identity and Dispensationalist Protestantism. By his reading we were in the sixth of history's seven ages. America would fragment into warring racial and ethnic fiefdoms, like Lebanon or Somalia. Whites would emerge victorious, God's kingdom would be established on earth for 1,000 years, the "Millenial Dispensation."

His political campaign, whatever its divine significance, engendered the wrath of Attorney General Robert Kennedy. "He set five agencies on me," Harrell says, "the IRS, the Federal Trade Commission, the Secret Service, . . . you name it." At the time, Harrell had established an armed religious settlement on his property, an entity he called the Christian Conservative Church of America, a refuge perhaps, but also a tax dodge. He says he gave sanctuary to a young man, 18-year-old Dion Davis, who turned out to be a military deserter. What the federal government did next, Harrell says, was the first step toward the Branch Davidian massacre in Waco.

It was also a simpler, less violent world. "They come in at 4:00 a.m. ('Look it up in the papers, it made headlines!') on Friday, August 4, 1961. With a hundred troopers and FBI agents and aircraft overhead. An Army half-track crashed through the front gate. Wrecked three automobiles. They eventually sent the boy home and charged me with harboring a Marine deserter. I got a ten-year jail sentence."

According to news reports at the time, Harrell had not filed income tax returns since 1953. Also, in March 1964, he jumped bail and disappeared. He was arrested 18 months later, hiding in an Arkansas farmhouse. He went to prison for four years, serving time in the federal penitentiaries in Terre Haute and Leavenworth.

In prison he developed the "expertise" to understand black people. "I know more about 'em than most folk," he says. "I've walked hundreds of miles, ate scores of meals with them. I slept where I could touch them in the night. How many nights have you spent with blacks? How many meals? How many days have you spent with them in a cell on both sides of you?"

Credentials established, Harrell lays out the sum of his racial theories: "Sexually, blacks are more animalistic." And not all people who call themselves black are black. "Andrew Young's not black," Harrell says. "Jesse Jackson's not black! Muhammad Ali's not black."

Now he leans close to me, wanting to share a story man to man.

"When I was in prison," he says, "I was with a real nice fellow. He was serving time for transporting women across state lines for immoral purposes. A pimp. He talked about what his various customers liked and wanted.

"He said, 'Jews got it beat like you never saw. A Jew wants to suck the semen out of a woman that's had relations with another man. It was so prevalent, the girls would run out of semen. We'd take an egg white and put salt on it and a little Clorox and you inject it into her.'

"Ain't that fan-tastic!"

Understand, Johnny Bob Harrell is a moral man. As he talks, I glance at a sheet listing the dress code for one of his Freedom Festivals. He spelled it right out: *No halter tops for those 12 years or older.*

I ask Harrell to show me his camp. And he agrees. We walk into an oak longhouse containing offices, rest rooms, a women's dormitory. Outside, birdhouses sit on tall posts. Everything is primitive and hand-built, the wood cut at a sawmill across the road. He's also building an airstrip back in the woods, a base for a civilian air force he claims he's assembling. "This is a distribution center," he says, "same as any other business."

One of his sons and some workers are pouring concrete for what Harrell describes as a new chapel and a dormitory. One of the sweating men is named John Smith. He's dressed in bib overalls and a straw hat, as American as the soil I'm standing on. Harrell begins his anti-Semitic rant again. John Smith nods in vigorous agreement at the things Harrell is telling me. To my surprise, a deep sadness sweeps over me. I want John Smith to be clean and pure as the corn in the fields.

"There's two kinds of Jews," Harrell says. "The Zionist is a parasite, anti-Christ, anti-Christian . . . lice and moles and cockroaches . . . against prayer in school, the nativity scene, Easter. The Zionist is a parasite, you find him where's there's narcotics, pornography, in the movie business. He goes for the jugular. You got to get up early to get ahead of him. Like trying to sneak morning past the rooster. It can't hardly be done.

"The little Jew gets hurt like everybody else. They'll blow him up with a bomb as quick as anyone else."

"I see."

We walk back to his office. Maps are pinned to the wall like some great military maneuver is about to begin. Harrell sits down heavily. His foot tap-tap-tapping as he talks. Otherwise, he shows no emotion. We might be discussing the price of corn. His anti-Semitism is a given, part of an old tradition, as American as Henry Ford. In the thirties and forties, pillars of the Old Christian Right—William Pelley, Gerald Winrod, Gerald L. K. Smith—preached the same rot and millions listened. Tens of thousands died because the heartland anti-Semites and their political allies in Congress closed the door to Jewish immigrants trying to escape Hitler's ovens.

"Johnny Bob," I ask, "how can you tell the little Jew from the Zionist?"

"There's things I just know," he says. "You can argue, fuss, yell and scream. When it's all over I just know. When you know, you know."

Harrell insists his beliefs are part of his rural heritage. He pops a tape of the song "A Country Boy Will Survive," plays it and looks at me to be sure I'm getting its "meaning."

"You're gonna find this song to be true," he says, getting up as I start to walk out the door to my car. "We've got guns, we're independent. We're out of touch with reality."

"That's the truth," I mumble.

"Don't make no difference what you write," he says. "We benefit from the worst kind of story."

He gestures at the green hills, the forests and blue sky swirling above him. "This is paradise," he says, "Literal paradise. Remember out here, you count for something!"

"I'll remember." In fact, I want to believe him.

When I leave, pushing my Toyota south toward the Gulf of Mexico, hundreds of police officers are involved in a manhunt for a white sociopath named (oddly enough) Michael Jackson, who's cut a swath of murder and mayhem across Indiana and Missouri. Thousands of terrified folk are barricaded in their houses. I'm stopped three times by state troopers hunting Jackson, who, thankfully, shoots himself as the cops close in.

Bay St. Louis, Mississippi

It's hot in Mississippi. The Gulf of Mexico is flat and bright as a silver dollar, the air humid, ripe with the smell of decaying fish. Vietnamese boat people-turned-Gulf Coast shrimpers repair nets on the rickety docks. The older ones are still dressed in broad-brimmed hats and pajamas, their teeth stained red from chewing betel nuts. On Ballantine Street, looking for another of God's Dragons, I find an old man sound asleep in a garage. Snoring, at peace.

A man who in 1990 counseled America's patriots: "When God Almighty took his people to the Promised Land, He told them to enter the land and kill every man, woman, child and suckling living thing there. . . . God knew that someday He would hear His people say, 'But some of them are my best friends!' God said, 'Kill every one of them.'"

Advice, as I write these words, that someone has just taken to heart in Atlanta's Centennial Olympic Park.

I stare down at this man, the willing architect of much hatred and dissension. He's short, squat, bald, at least 70 years old. This is "Brigadier General" Jack Mohr, an inveterate anti-Semite who's bounced around the fringe for decades, like a Catskills comedian waiting for his big break.

A wicked-looking double-barrelled shotgun leans against the wall, so I'm hesitant to disturb the guy's slumber. I walk over to a wood-frame house with a tiny garden out front and knock on the door. A ratty van parked in the driveway is plastered with NRA stickers. I introduce myself to Mohr's wife, Doris, who shoots me a sour look then escorts me back to the garage to awaken the sleeping general.

He yawns and stretches. I notice he's wearing a hearing aid. His desk is surrounded by stacks of pamphlets and poorly printed newsletters, *The Plot Against Christianity*, *The Thirteenth Tribe*, *You Gentiles*, *White Power*, *The Talmud*, *The New Jewish Encyclopedia*, among them. Remembering my run-in with Slim Parrino, I ask about the shotgun.

"The Jewish Defense League," he says, "has got a contract out on me."

"I see."

In the fifties, Mohr, an army officer, had a life-changing experience. He claims he was captured and tortured by North Korean communists, barely escaping the firing squad. When he retired from the military, he became a member of the John Birch Society's Speakers Bureau, traveling the country in the sixties and seventies to spread the Birchers' anti-Communist gospel. In the late seventies, he quit to link up with John Harrell's Civilian Emergency Defense System.

Through the eighties, as far-right rhetoric turned violent and revolutionary, Mohr was everywhere, a tough-talking, self-proclaimed expert on everything—assault weapons, propaganda, espionage, conspiracy, Judaism, anthropology—mingling with far-right "elders" like Richard Butler, William Potter Gale, Pete Peters, John Harrell and Michigan Klan leader Robert Miles. His "beliefs," spewed out in speeches and far-right periodicals—*The Christian Patriot Crusader, The Klansman, Aryan Nations' Newsletter,* the *Christian Vanguard Newsletter*—were ever more rabid.

The man I'm staring at is feeble as a baby, his life sustained by a pacemaker implanted in his chest. Again, I wonder how many hearts and minds the old soldier has reached. How many self-proclaimed captains and colonels in God's armies have imagined marching alongside the far right's fabled "Brigadier General"? A rank, by the way, he never held in the military.

And I ask myself, what am I doing here?

I'm not going to sit for another harangue about international conspirators and "mud races," not after all these months. Not with my children just a day's drive east. After ascertaining—however he did it—I was a Christian journalist, Mohr pulls out a letter written, he tells me, by one Jan

Beaderstadt, editor of *The Daily News* in Iron Mountain, Michigan. It reads, in part:

> We are using our newspaper to make the people think what we want them to think . . . so the citizens will turn in their guns, because our editorials and stories show how dangerous they are. This is our mission in the Upper Peninsula. There are no open Jews, none of our Black brothers like to come up here because of the cold. So when the time comes, it may be harder for us to subjugate the white people who have not joined our cause, unless they turn in their guns.
>
> We laugh at you now. Why not give up? We are in control of everything that matters. A whole generation has been raised on our message on TV. They like Black shows. We have convinced them all that Israel is our best friend in the Middle East. Everyone, including the Whites, think what we have taught them to. Foolish people like you who fight the trend will get nowhere.
>
> Why not join us. I was not a Jew until I got into the newspaper trade. Then I saw what it would take to get ahead and [I] converted. The blood ritual is simple and relatively painless. Are you man enough to take it? On the other hand, if you continue to defy us, that serves our purposes well. We can point to people like you and say, "There is freedom of the press still." You play right into our hands.
>
> Become a Jew. Take the easy way out. Have you ever touched a black woman? It is a wonderful sex experience which can be yours if you convert. You can share your seed with White men or Black ones too, when you are with us. Consider it seriously.

Mohr's chin is bobbing as I read the letter.

"Well, Vincent, what do you think of that?"

"Jack, it's hard to believe," I say, getting up to leave.

"I know, but every word is true."

Needless to say, editor Hap Rondeau and the other folks I spoke to when I called the *Daily News* in Iron Mountain, Michigan, had never heard of Mr. Jan Beaderstadt.

A few years later, Jack Mohr announced his health had forced him to leave the struggle to younger men. He would continue, he said, to put out his tracts, books and tapes "on conspiracy and Bible truths" from his home.

And continue, no doubt to sleep peacefully.

In 1995, 73-year-old John Harrell was broke, living on Social Security benefits, claiming to own nothing more than "some socks, some shirts and an old Ford." The "Mount Vernon" homestead, 100 miles east of St. Louis, was overgrown with weeds and in disrepair, its guardhouse piled with trash. His "air force" a rusting plane squatting naked in a field.

After the Oklahoma City bombing, reporters on the trail of Timothy McVeigh and Terry Nichols tracked Harrell down. He claims he never heard of either of them, though he also believes the bombing was the work of an administration in Washington "that will do almost anything to gain its ends."

Most days, Harrell shuffles around the decayed mansion, stuffing and mailing envelopes containing dire warnings that the republic is about to be overwhelmed. On the homefront he has suffered another humiliating defeat: one of his daughters married a black man.

"I'm tired of it all," he says.

I agree.

We met at the top of a bank in Dallas in a fancy dining room. There were priests drinking, the chairman of the board sat with a young blonde. They ridiculed my thesis.

—Larry Humphreys, the Heritage Library

Chapter 11

Confusion's Masterpiece

Velma, Oklahoma

No one will ever confuse Larry Humphreys with Martin Luther. Among the fried and freeze-dried in Vail, Colorado, Humphreys is remembered as the mostly stoned owner of the Red Cock Rooster Farm, a restaurant he drove into bankruptcy with the speed of a downhill racer. "Hell, I carried this big ol' bag of cocaine with me," he says, remembering the bad old days, "and I was chasing all the horny schoolteachers."

When I find him, Humphreys is a stone-sober vegetarian

living with an Aryan wife in southern Oklahoma on 3,000 acres he inherited from his father, an oil and banking tycoon. He's quite handsome, with features that recall Montgomery Clift, only taller and kind of country-goofy.

No paradise, this town of Velma (population 611). The air is heavy with the stench of raw petroleum, the streets cracked and broken. Pumpjacks are everywhere, in pastures and front yards, across the street from the Velma-Alma High School, with its faded sign commemorating the Comets' Class B Track Championship.

Larry's father didn't marry until his sixties, when he felt financially secure enough to start a family; Larry, his only son, couldn't spend money fast enough. In Vail, he'd catch the plane to Vegas two or three times a month to burn up the line of credit he'd gotten as an 18th birthday present.

He'd been packed off in his teens to New Jersey's Garland School for Boys, an ivory-towered reformatory for wayward rich kids. On holidays, he'd return to Oklahoma, baggies of marijuana stuffed in his luggage, eager "to turn my friends on to drugs." His father was in his seventies before Larry was ten years old. The boy's bluster was mostly an act, a cover for his loneliness. "Notice me!" Larry shouted. "Love me!" he whispered. It was too late. All too soon his father was dead.

He dropped out of Oklahoma University after one drunken semester. His father had hoped his son would follow his footsteps and become a banker; Larry dreamed of becoming the world's greatest pool shark. Bankrolled by a seemingly bottomless trust fund—$500,000, with payments coming every two years—Humphreys had crisscrossed the dives and juke joints of Oklahoma and Texas with his mentor, a black pimp, he says, from Houston. "I've played in a lot of bars," Humphreys tells me, "and took out all the money."

By his late twenties, the alcohol, the blow, the rainbow of pills began to blur his thinking, unsteady his hand. His friends, guys who'd struggled back to Oklahoma from 'Nam, had had it right: life wasn't nothing but a thing. Humphreys was sucking on a tequila bottle, doing about 90 mph, when the railroad abutment whispered to him. He survived the head-on crash, but emptiness bled from his wounds.

"I feel a burden," he says of those years. "The end of my ways. I'm looking at the people I'm associating with, feeling responsibility to my land, my estate, the need for some kind of moral existence. My father was a Christian pillar of the community. I decided to return."

He's telling me these things as we stand in front of what may be the masterpiece of his confusion: The Heritage Library, a moldy collection of pro-Nazi, anti-Communist, racist and anti-Semitic literature, a malignancy budding in the prairie's heart.

Humphreys' library sits in a stand of willow, pecan and red-bud trees about a mile from downtown Velma. The road leading to the place circles a lovely man-made lake and crosses a small bridge monitored by a crude electronic security system. The building is circular, constructed of stone and glass, topped by a shingled conical roof. On 14 flagpoles flutter the standards of northern Europe's Aryan Nations. Nearby is Larry's modest A-frame house.

Twenty yards from the library is a swimming pool dimpled by frogs, its landscaped flowers and potted plants overgrown and tangled. Exercise equipment, a tattered pool table, bar and components of a very expensive stereo system lie rotting in an oversized pool house, its showers reeking of mildew. A bird's nest is precariously perched on top of the pool house's open door.

Humphreys came back to Oklahoma to recuperate after the car crash. He dried out working as a field hand on his own land. Stayed celibate, he says, for a year and a half. He began attending the local Baptist church, was born again, baptized with his own tears in the arms of a missionary from North

Carolina named Bertha Smith. He plunged into his newfound faith, eager for the same rush he felt when he snorted cocaine. It wasn't there. "Something was missing," he says. He began searching, visiting odd Christian sects that were springing up like mushrooms across the Midwest. Delving into biblical prophecy. "The Anti-Christ, the One World System," he discovered, "have all been foretold."

Ever the adrenalin junkie, he plunged deeper, learning, he says, hidden things about his ancestors. Things more important than the sweat, the sodbusting and wildcatting that had made his daddy rich and his life easy. Astounding things. Thousands of years before those sturdy Angles, Saxons and Jutes ever reached the coasts of England, they'd lived in the Holy Land. They were the true Israelites. According to God's will they were scattered, banished across the Caucasus Mountains and into Europe. Over the long centuries, Satanic impostors had seized his birthright, propelling the world on a long spin into chaos.

Larry Humphreys had found his Identity.

"My eyes opened and my feet didn't hit the ground," he says. "All my questions were answered. Why is there social injustice? A decline in our national fiber? As people of the Book, we're charged with administering God's laws. We've failed."

Here was a truth even his daddy hadn't understood. A challenge this prodigal son could pursue. Unfortunately, it was the other Larry Humphreys, the loudmouthed, rambunctious, goofy one who went off to battle. He began challenging the preachers in the Baptist churches in Velma, Alma, all the way to Lawton. Country pastors who'd raised and praised him, who'd lived off his daddy's tithes, he now reviled as Pharisees. He used his family name to set up a meeting with Baptist elders at the Dallas Theological Seminary.

It was a humiliation he says he'll never forget: "We met in the top of a bank in Dallas in a fancy formal dining room.

There were preachers drinking. The chairman of the board sat with a young blonde. They . . . they ridiculed my thesis." Back home, Humphreys was branded a heretic, yo-yo and cow patty. The long-haired kids hanging out at Billie's Quick Sak convenience store hooted as he drove by. Old folks, displaying raggedy goods in front-yard sales, looked the other way.

So be it. Larry Humphreys would build a monument to the Truth. He would document the glories of the white race in a heritage library that he envisioned would be a combination Aryan memorial and research center. He opened his checkbook, dispensing money like a pope: $1.3 million in construction costs, $200,000 to start the *American Heritage* magazine, a publication he hoped would spread the news of the library. He bought typewriters, office equipment, paid salaries to staff members. He hired the redoubtable Mrs. William Lent, Senator Joe McCarthy's secretary, to be his librarian. Then he forked over another $300,000 for a lumber operation to keep the scores of extremists who began to show up gainfully employed.

Basking in the attention of tough-talking men—Klansman Louis Beam, Order founder Bob Matthews, and an odd young man who claimed to be the son of the famed airline hijacker D. W. Cooper, among them—Humphreys tore the license plates off his cars, howling defiance at bewildered local deputies who'd known him since he was a boy. He replaced the plates with the American flag, stockpiled weapons, began militia-style training on the ranch.

While Larry Humphreys chased his dream, the scruffy Aryans hung around, playing soldier, getting stoned by the swimming pool, bragging about shooting FBI agents and the young women they'd fucked. Humphreys' investment in the lumber business went up in smoke. The Aryans slunk off when Larry's wife, who detested the foul-looking, leering men who gravitated like flies to Velma, ordered the checkbook closed. "Freeloaders," scoffs Bill Hight, an old radical who works as

Humphreys' gardener and caretaker. "None of 'em weren't worth a shit."

Humphreys turned his attention to the small farmers and ranchers all around him, men beaten to their knees by soaring debt and falling prices, struggling to hang on to their land. In the ultimate analysis, he decided, the farmers could be a powerful force—they controlled the nation's food supply—no bank or army would stand against.

"Defending life and property is biblical and constitutional," Larry is telling me, when his wife, Katherine Vegsund, calls him inside for lunch.

"Our last check and balance."

Lunch must be interesting, given the fact we're in south Oklahoma, where the oil wells are outnumbered only by the number of junk-food palaces and greasy spoons, and Katherine, who grew up in an ultra-orthodox Identity Christian sect in the Pacific Northwest, observes Kosher dietary laws. She also celebrates a Saturday Sabbath, and the Feasts of Tabernacles and Trumpets instead of Christmas and Easter.

Vegsund, a very attractive lady, read about Humphreys— the rare Aryan millionaire!—in a movement newspaper; she quit a secretarial job in Eureka, California, and headed straight to Oklahoma. The two fell in love and were married in less than a year. "He's married to me," Katherine insisted, "but he's married to America first."

I'm left standing there. The sun is blinding, spots begin dancing in front of my eyes. I walk inside, under the wilting semicircle of flags, to visit the library I'd driven a thousand miles to see, a place I'd imagined a thousand times. It's deserted, musty. A brass plaque near the entrance explains that its collections "deal with the conspiracy of history theory, the idea that there is a small group of super-powerful and wealthy individuals who, from behind the scenes, control the destinies of men and nations."

I walk among the racks, past reference materials and dictionaries any high school library would have. A closer look turns up rows of benign-sounding Identity books like *Anglo Saxon Superiority*, by Edward Demolins; *Britain and America—The Lost Israelites*, by Reverend P. S. McKillop; *The Wonder Race*, by Mrs. G. E. Altree. And then other books, less benign, *The International Jew* . . . *The Myth of the Six Million* . . . *The Plot Against Christianity* . . . *The Kabbalah 1865* . . . *The Red Flag Over America* . . . *The Ku Klux Klan* . . . *With Hitler on the Road to Power*, by Otto Dietrich.

I pick up *Jugend um Hitler*, an old photo essay of a smiling, fatherly führer posing with the handsome, fair-haired children of his Reich. Page after page. I throw it down.

Dozens of newsletters and hate sheets are piled on tables. I pick up *Identity: The Association of the Covenant People*. It contains an article on AIDS titled "A Queer Phenomenon: The Curse on Defiant Lawlessness." My kid brother Thomas, a very good man, suffered horribly and died of AIDS. He was 28 years old. I'm beginning to comprehend how a person could burn down a library. An issue of something called the *National Vanguard* defends Josef Mengele and goes on to praise Middle East terrorists for "converting Israeli soldiers to good Jews."

A poster inside a copy of a rag called the *National Socialist Observer* proclaims, "The Future Belongs to the Few of Us Willing to Get Our Hands Dirty."

The Alfred P. Murrah Federal Building in Oklahoma City is just 100 miles north of where I'm standing.

After awhile I have to stop taking notes. Many of these books have been donated from other collections and bear loving inscriptions. Some are written by women; others obviously intended for children. The minds that wrote this stuff. The lives they must have led. The gods they worshiped. Humphreys' library is an open grave, festering in the bright Oklahoma sun. The ghosts of its victims, whose very suffering it denies and mocks, whirl and moan in the air.

"Got to get out of here," I tell myself, feeling suffocated. I want to breathe, call somebody far away.

That night I drive back into Velma with Katherine, who needs to buy some baby food. "They think we're cultists, murdering babies," she tells me as we drive through town. "But when Christ returns, this library will be crowded with believers." She pauses, fixes me with her ice-blue eyes and whispers, "You do know Larry is being used by God?"

"Yeah, I can see that," I say backing away.

I while away a long hot afternoon, talking to folks hanging around the Billie's Quik-Stop convenience store. Teenagers, cops, the waitress, no one has much empathy for Mr. Humphreys; the library might as well be Frankenstein's Castle. I grab some dinner, look for a movie. The nearest one is in Lawton, too many miles away. There are no hotels in Velma, so I'm forced to go back to the library where I spend a restless night in the library's "Dan, Asher, Naphtali Guest Room," expecting the locals to torch the place with me inside.

In the morning, I walk outside and find Humphreys, now dressed in what look like fancy tennis clothes, lounging by the stagnant pool talking to a rawboned man with a cowboy hat on his lap. After a minute, Humphreys waves me over.

"Jack, this is Vince . . . Copa . . . What was that?"

"Vince Coppola. . . . I'm a writer, doing a little story on Larry."

"Jack Stone," he says, crunching my extended hand. "Got a ranch not far from here." His hand drifts to the pocket of his western shirt, shakes out a cigarette from a pack of Lucky Strikes. My father's old brand. I haven't seen one in years.

"Mind if I sit in?" I ask.

"Sure, not a problem. Got nothing to hide."

Stone had leased his land to some oil and gas interests who had made a strike. Now he complained he was getting screwed. The contracts were vague and ill-defined. The courts and his own lawyers had done nothing. He suspected they had conspired against him. He tells the story slowly; shame, anger, and what I take to be a kind of midwestern reticence, all warring within him.

"The same thing that's happening to me, happened to 400 ranchers in Montana," Stone says. "People are losing control of their own property."

Humphreys nods his head sagely like Solomon. He counsels Stone to consult the library's videotaped collection of Common Law and *pro se* legal strategies. I've seen these before, with Derral Schroder and others, useless instruments in a farmer's battles to save his land. Using prepackaged, often expensive do-it-yourself kits, a man can argue that the interest charged on his mortgage was usury, forbidden by the Bible and English Common Law, upon which our judicial system is based. Such a loan is therefore invalid and foreclosure proceedings unenforceable. I try to imagine a harried judge ruling in favor of such arguments. At best, they slow things up, by clogging the system. At worst, they're rip-offs by con men posing as patriots.

"I don't know how to express myself," says Stone, chain-smoking another Lucky. "I'm not familiar with different types of law. But I know right from wrong, just from unjust!"

"Have you done any research on zoning?" says Humphreys.

What the hell's that got to do with it? I'm thinking.

"Not really," says Stone. "Who knows what the law is? It's an absurd, grotesque deal. I don't get along with attorneys. I hate 'em."

"And the banks," says Humphreys, "they literally commit fraud in their greed for collateral."

I'm confused.

Stone's nodding in agreement. "My lawyer is making a lot more money," he says, "making sure I lose than helping me win!"

I realize these guys aren't talking, just making what in other times would be empty speeches, two guys blowing off steam. Humphreys next begins to outline a legal strategy so unfathomable, I stop taking notes.

"I think you can still go back and recover," he tells Stone, who's as bewildered as I am.

"It's the destruction of private ownership" (Humphreys is on a roll). "In the last ten years it's accelerated at a fantastic rate. Read the first ten planks of the *Communist Manifesto* about taking personal property!"

"Larry—" I start to say.

"I've been raped in the courts like all the rest," Stone cuts in. "I've got more beefs that Iowa Packing."

"Larry . . ."

Humphreys glances at his watch. Gets up, looks toward the A-frame where the lovely Katherine is no doubt waiting for him. "The land of the free and the home of the brave," he says, nodding good-bye to Stone and me. "With liberty and justice for all!"

With that, Jack Stone picked up his black Stetson and made his way uncertainly into the library's Gordon Kahl Memorial Wing. For the next two days I watched him, a decent man, sit sweating in a corner of the library vainly trying to master the intricacies of Common Law, debt cancellation and the Land Sabbath.

The "Land Sabbath," as I would soon learn, is Larry Humphreys' answer to America's farm crisis and, by extension, many of the other economic ills plaguing the country. He says he found it in the Scriptures (Deuteronomy 15:1-2). All land is to be left fallow, and all debts forgiven every seven years.

"What are you talking about, Larry?" I ask. "Who would ever go for that?"

He doesn't hear a word I say.

"The president of the United States could say, 'If the farmers don't want to get off the land, we're not going to push 'em off!' I don't know what the legal basis would be, but think of the psychological impact!"

I'm thinking, "A bullshit artist."

A year later, I see Larry Humphreys in Georgia. He's holding a SWAT team at bay with a sawed-off shotgun. Scores of reporters and photographers are milling around behind a barricade. I'm one of them. Humphreys' handsome face is being transmitted by satellite around the world.

Larry and four heavily armed followers have come out of the West to make a stand. "We're prepared to die," Larry announces, fingering the shotgun. Clearly he wasn't bullshitting this time.

In Oklahoma, he'd prepared 300 videotapes and shipped them out to patriot and militia groups all over the country. On the tape, he promised to "stand with the first man who would defend his land."

Word came back from an American Agriculture Movement organizer in middle Georgia named Tommy Kirsey about a hog farmer named Oscar Lorick who was about to be evicted. Lorick owed the Cook Banking Company $112,000 on a farm worth $90,000. There are thousands of similar stories—Humphreys had a dozen evictions to choose from—but Oscar's had its own special shame and resonance. Lorick is black, his ancestors had struggled up from slavery on this land. A farm paid for with 120 years of sweat and tears would be lost with the stroke of a pen.

I see Lorick, a bear of a man, in his seventies, confused, hesitant, seemingly ready to cry. The bankers, he whispers, had told him "twisty things." He'd put his mark on their paper, borrowed money he had never seen to settle debts he didn't remember running up. Now they were taking his house and his last remaining acreage. "That ain't right," he drawled. "No suh!"

As it turned out, Humphreys' fatigue-clad men are ordinary, middle-class guys—today's militias are cut from the same cloth—with wives, families and mortgages. If anything, they said they considered themselves not more militant but more idealistic than their neighbors. One, Jerry Giesbecht, is a gunsmith. Another, Jerry Vandevur, manufactures dentures. Gary Williamson works as an electrician.

As the hour approached for Bleckley County sheriff Ed Coley to come evict Lorick, Humphreys set up a symbolic "perimeter" of hay bales and string, vowing to reporters and gawking locals that Oscar would not be moved. Coley, who wanted the whole mess to go away, began delaying. Humphreys, who was proving much more media savvy than I'd credited him for, was hoping to force Georgia's governor, Joe Frank Harris, into declaring a "state of insurgency."

Such a declaration, Humphreys reasoned, would propel the farm crisis and, with it, Larry Humphreys, former owner of the Red Cock Rooster Farm, into the national spotlight.

The Lorick episode was before the Waco, Texas, conflagration with the Branch Davidians, before the debacle on Ruby Ridge, but already a handful of desperate farmers had died under the guns of federal agents. Men who died believing they were defending their wives and children, their very birthright. The stories flew like tumbleweeds across the prairies.

Kirsey, a hardbitten organizer who had participated in the tractorcades that rolled on Washington in the seventies, had 40 armed men waiting in a barn half a mile away. Visions of Bunker Hill danced in Larry Humphreys' head. And martyrdom as sure as any Shiite. "If I die," he told me, "I'm assured the promise of eternal life."

Ed Coley was too smart to give him his chance. He'd been a country sheriff far too long. The national media was hanging on Humphreys' every word. Pictures of the fatigue-clad Giesbecht cradling an assault rifle, of Oscar in his bib overalls, of his pretty grandchildren, were flashing around the country. None of this was good news for Coley, a man who wanted to finish his term in office without incident and collect his pension. Now the NAACP was rallying to Lorick's cause. And here was this outside agitator—a white supremacist no less—helping a black farmer! Coley huddled with state and federal negotiators; he fired off messages to the bankers, to the governor.

And then backed down.

The eviction was stopped right there on the courthouse steps. A crowd of jubilant farmers whooped and hollered as Katherine rushed to Larry's side and hugged him. Oscar wound up in People magazine, his debts paid by tens of thousands of dollars in donations that poured in from around the country.

Late that night, I watched the Oklahomans melt away into the mist; they would return again in the nineties, marching under different banners, their ranks and their anger multiplied a hundredfold.

I tracked Humphreys' career over the years. In the late eighties he was so broke his mother had to pay his electric bills. She'd ordered him to return to Dallas and enroll in engineering school if he wanted to eat. I saw him in Missouri at a gathering of the paramilitary Christian Patriots Defense League, ranting about the Land Sabbath and the unholy forces that were conspiring against America. He was planning to run for Congress.

He liked to retell the Lorick story. "I proved the government can't run roughshod over people," he said. "The next time we're gonna involve hundreds of people. We're gonna do it right."

As I was packing to leave the gloom of the library, Noah Tuttle, another of the library's caretakers, knocked softly on my door. A big man, well into his sixties, Noah was a Baptist preacher

who'd been defrocked for espousing Identity Christianity. He'd
sat in one of my interviews with Humphreys, never speaking a
word. He puffed on his pipe and smiled self-consciously if I
looked his way. When it was over, he said reporters sometimes
distorted truth. He hoped I'd be fair.

Two hours later he was back. He had been unchristian, he
decided. Would I accept his apology? It was easier to say 'yes'
than suggest he was overreacting. He invited me to Sunday
morning breakfast. Wracked by months of loneliness, suspicion
and distrust, I accepted. In the morning, he drove me to the
stand of trees that shaded his double-wide trailer. Elva, his wife,
had been up for hours preparing the meal. Everything was fresh
or homemade, new eggs and country sausage, biscuits, milk from
the ranch's goats, Elva's plum and apricot jellies, honey from the
hive. They fussed over me like grandparents with a six-year-old.
I realized they were lonely, too.

After breakfast I followed them to a Christian Fellowship
service in Velma. The church was a storefront crowded with
folding chairs, the service chaotic compared to the precise ritu-
als of Catholicism. Children huddled with crayons and coloring
books on the floor; toddlers crawled beneath the seats. One little girl munched a candy bar, her younger brother kept trying
to snatch it away. Musicians banged away on drums and guitars.

They sang hymns, the words scrawled on an overhead pro-
jector. As the music washed over me, I began to tremble. My
younger brother had died some months before. His death
haunted me. He'd never traveled, never seen much of the
world. I wished he were beside me. I knew these people would
have comforted him. I began to sob.

A couple moved to the front row and took seats on separate
sides of the aisle. Men and women walked up and sat beside
them, men next to the husband, women with the wife. They
whispered and embraced. A great sobbing filled the room. It
was like the sacrament of Confession, only public, with real
shoulders to cry on.

Noah, so meek in private, bellowed joyful "Hallelujahs," and "Say Ons." Elva, raising her hands in an evangelical salute, sang her hymns with the sweetest, purest voice.

Outside, I was introduced around. Strangers pumped my hand, said they hoped I'd find whatever I was looking for. I tried to tell them I had.

Conclusion

One Hundred Percent Americanism

The past, I'm learning, holds the key to the present. CSA, The Order, the Posse Comitatus and the militias did not spring full blown out of the air. David Tate was not born a killer.

The Dragons had been rampant before.[1] Their trail leads at

---

1. One of the most thorough analyses of right-wing extremism in the earlier 20th century is Leo P. Ribuffo's *The Old Christian Right*, a work that provided many of the historical guideposts for my journey.

least as far back as the turn of the century. An Anglo-Saxon elite watched as eastern and southern European immigrants poured into the cities. It wasn't the babbling tongues and desperate poverty of the newcomers. They were aliens, thus unable to comprehend the bedrock virtues—industry, piety, fair play—upon which the nation was supposedly founded.

These Anglo-Saxons, calling themselves *nativists*, used pseudo-scientific research to pronounce the immigrants degenerate species, incapable of assimilation. Worse, they would bore like termites into the foundations of the republic and bring it crashing down. Madison Grant's bestselling The *Passing of the Great Race* was hailed by businessmen, politicians, scientists and scholars.

In the 1890s, the American Protective Association (APA), a secret society boasting 500,000 members, demanded that Catholics be barred from public office and prevented from teaching in public schools. Bogus "ex-priests" and "nuns" exposed the lurid secrets of the cloistered life: the Pope planned to make America his fiefdom. Anti-Catholic harassment continued through the 1920s; the Ku Klux Klan spent as much of its venom on popery as on blacks.

Jews were particular targets. The nativists drew on a tradition that stretched back 2,000 years. Jews had been condemned in the New Testament; they'd been denounced by Martin Luther himself. Christ's blood was on their hands. Anti-Semitic motifs appeared in the literature of Chaucer and Shakespeare and continued on down to the dime novel.

Jews, said the nativists, lacked the sturdy Anglo-Saxon virtues, which paradoxically, were associated with Old Testament Hebrews. They were greedy, unscrupulous, immoral, pitiless. The Christian was patriotic, the Jew loyal only to his fellows. Jews were cunning; they spread ideas like viruses.

The Bolshevik Revolution provoked a Red Scare that consolidated free-floating intolerance into systematic hatemongering. In works like *The Protocols of the Learned Elders of Zion*, suspicions became detailed conspiracies. Jewish villains emerged: Bernard Baruch, who forced through the Federal Reserve Act and "placed the banking reserves of the nation under the control of Jewish international bankers"; Supreme Court justice Felix Frankfurter, who placed "many Reds in government."

Supporters of the Klan, the American Defense Society and other vigilance groups numbered in the millions. "One Hundred Percent Americanism" echoed from the drawing room to the street corner. These radicals were suddenly everywhere—in the churches, the universities, the union halls, the ghettos. Jews found themselves inextricably linked with communism.

Fundamentalist Christianity has been linked to anti-Semitism, but many turn-of-the-century fundamentalists were ambivalent. Some regarded Jews as God's Chosen People. Others believed Semitic mischief was part of God's plan.

Dispensationalists—Christian Patriots Defense League founder John Harrell is a modern example—believed Jews had a great prophecy to fulfill. History was divided into seven ages. Man was in the final hours of a corrupt age. The Beast (Anti-Christ) prophesied in Revelation would soon appear and restore the Roman Empire. Jews would ally with the Beast and return to Jerusalem, setting the stage for Christ's Second Coming. Christ would defeat the Beast at the battle of Armageddon, a victory that signaled the start of the Millennium—the thousand years' reign of Christ that precedes the Last Judgment.

World War I and the peacetime excesses of the 1920s were proof to many that Armageddon was at hand. Battered by spiritual and economic storms, America drifted without compass into the Depression. Millions may have supported Franklin Roosevelt's reforms, but millions more saw Jews manipulating New Deal policies.

A handful of popular figures—Father Charles Coughlin, Gerald Winrod, William Pelley, Gerald L. K. Smith—provided a fascist counterpoint to the New Deal. They set the stage for today's extremists, mouthing the same hollow pieties (hard work, discipline, rectitude, revival) and the same violent and divisive rhetoric.

They commanded paramilitary forces composed of men eager to brutalize Reds, union organizers, immigrants. William Pelley, the mystic (spirits informed him that Jews corrupted the white civilization of Atlantis), founded the Silver Legion. Coughlin, a Catholic priest, reached millions with his virulently anti-Semitic radio broadcasts before being reined in by his bishop. Winrod founded the Defenders of the Christian Faith; Smith was a disciple of populist Huey Long.

Thin support faded as Americans got a better look at Hitler, Franco and Mussolini. Industrialists who'd offered encouragement and financial assistance in return for union bashing began backpedaling. As America moved toward World War II, the radicals became increasingly isolated, though still embraced by out-and-out Nazis and collaborators.

Pelley openly praised Hitler. Like today's Identity Christians, he envisioned a nation he called "Christ State," where blacks would be prevented from mating with white women and Jews would be under the control of an Aryan Secretary for Jewry. He claimed Machiavelli's *The Prince* was an early edition of the *Protocols*, citing secret sources and "missing pages" from the writings of Benjamin Franklin as proof.

Gerald Winrod decided the Anti-Christ would be a Jew.

Gerald Smith ran for president on a platform that promised to investigate whether the New Deal was "heavily staffed by a certain type of Jewish bureaucrat."

Winrod, Pelley and Smith were involved in a series of trials that dragged on during World War II. Franklin Roosevelt, long a target of fanatic venom, instigated the most significant, *United States v. McWilliams*. Charges brought against them ranged from inciting riot to participating in a worldwide Nazi conspiracy. None of the prosecutions was successful. These "Brown Scare" trials were notable, according to the defendants, for the left wing's willingness to deny the far right free speech. Ironically, the employment of innuendo, hearsay and exaggeration as evidence would be used much more successfully in Senator Joseph McCarthy's prosecution of the Left.

Far-right extremists waxed and waned through the 1950s and 1960s, creatures of cultural conflict and social change. The Cold War gave birth to the conspiracies of the John Birch Society and the paramilitary posturing of the Minutemen. Civil-rights protests breathed new life into the Ku Klux Klan. The Silver Shirts gave way to the storm troopers of George Lincoln Rockwell's American Nazi Party.

Goldwater loomed, then faded. Nixon and Agnew pandered. A barrage of threats—the New Left, gay rights, feminism, black nationalism, antiwar protests, Third World immigration—kept the patriots on their heels through the 1970s. For a time, even their symbols were co-opted: the swastika was favored by degenerate bikers and punks; Klan robes inspired mockery rather than terror. Today's skinheads wear Doc Martins and favor "romantic violence."

Even God seemed no longer on their side. Fundamentalists like Pat Robertson and Jerry Falwell have long rejected anti-Semitism, leaving the extremists to Identity Christianity's warlike embrace.

The cycles continue. America marched, out of step, through the 1980s. The first ranks moved with self-congratulatory smugness—*"The pride is back . . . "*—while the flanks swayed in disarray. The factories of the Rust Belt closed forever, a million farmers went bankrupt, schools systems crashed, inner cities rumbled. Corporate raiders swooped like vultures.

The 1990s have borne more bitter fruit: heroin addiction, violence, AIDS, child pornography, cults, gangs, domestic terror; the dearth of leadership, the death of hope, the curse of the militias. The fascists of the 1930s had not grown up with the rock-and-roll rhythms of automatic weapons. They had not been denied a livelihood because of Affirmative Action.

The call for a New Order has gone out again.

I see a greater dichotomy between rich and poor. A greater sense of racial awareness. Society will become more and more fragmented.

—David Duke, U.S. senatorial candidate, and
Former Klansman

I drove out of Velma in darkness so thick the twinkling lights on the oil rigs seemed ships afloat on an ocean of ink. Headlights of approaching vehicles were blinding, even at great distances. I stopped in Lawton to await the dawn.

Outside Lawton, the towns were so desolate even the pawnshops had closed. I passed a high school football field with scaling paint like snow on its bleachers. The sun blazed overhead. A solitary black athlete ran endlessly up and down the stadium steps.

After so many months, it was time to go home.

In this vast and familiar heartland, I'd seen a hundred subcultures, a thousand Americas both obscene and beautiful. Little girls won baseball games in small towns on mild summer nights, but vile hatred had survived intact for a hundred years.

Jews were still Christ-killers, the Catholic Church the Whore of Revelation. The Anti-Christ cast his monstrous shadow across the Plains. Armies massed, thirsting for war. In Oklahoma City and Waco, Texas, infants died choking on fire and smoke . . . Blacks were animals . . . Asians treacherous. Christ was a German, Bill Clinton a Jew.

When I arrived in Atlanta, the city was preparing to host the Centennial Olympic Games. A billion dollars, endless energy and good will had been spent fostering the evanescent dream that the world could be, however briefly, a civil and safe place.

A pipe dream, as it turned out.

At first, it was good to be home. "Back from the fringe," I told myself. Atlanta's booming development and aggressive self-promotion seemed familiar, almost innocent. My children greeted me, sweet Gabrielle waving a sheaf of wheat I'd sent her from Kansas, fair-haired Thomas clutching his GameBoy, excited about the "coffee grinder" dribble he'd mastered at basketball camp.

And then I remembered other children, other lives less blessed. In Waco and in Oklahoma City. In Denver, where accused Oklahoma City bombers Timothy McVeigh and Terry Nichols were to be tried, the wheels of justice ground slowly forward. With the trial, I hoped both rage and outrage would dissipate, sanity prevail.

Then I saw the smear of stories in the newspapers: soldiers of an ignorant army calling itself the Georgia Republic Militia had been arrested for conspiring to bomb federal buildings. In the twisted faces of these men—Robert Starr, Jimmy McCranie, Troy Allen Kyser—Robert Matthews, Jim Ellison, David Tate, David Dorr and Terry McVeigh came back to haunt me.

And then TWA Flight 800 exploded over New York City.

And the pipe-bomb went off in the Centennial Olympic Park.

And a woman lay dying. And the wounded shrieked. And the crowds fled in terror as we've seen so many times before.

Out there, I knew the Dragons were laughing, taking heart in the violence and flaring animosity. Pronouncing it "God's will." Again and again during my journey they had cheered the heroics of mainstream "white patriots" like Bernhard Goetz, the New York subway gunman who'd shot four black men he believed were about to mug him, who stood over one of the wounded and fired a second round into his spine.

In Idaho, I tried to tell David Dorr a story about Howard Beach in New York City. A story I'd covered as a reporter about three black men—Cedric Sandiford, Timothy Grimes and Michael Griffith—who had the misfortune of having their car break down on Cross Bay Boulevard, a thoroughfare running through the white, working-class neighborhood in the borough of Queens.

About the macho Italian and Irish teenagers who lived in Howard Beach. Klan robes and Nazi rhetoric were laughable to them, but cruelty and racism came easy, passed from father to son, visceral and explosive.

On foot, traveling through hostile territory, the men compounded their misfortune by exchanging insults with a group of white teenagers in a passing car. The youths were driving a girl home from a birthday party. The blacks stopped at the New York Pizzeria, unaware the whites had raced back to the party and called out nine others to hunt the intruders.

"Niggers, you don't belong here!" the teenagers shouted as they surrounded the trio. (It was a cry I'd heard a hundred times growing up in south Brooklyn.) They moved in, one boy wielded a baseball bat, another a tree limb. Grimes escaped, but Griffith and Sandiford were taken for sport. They were assaulted, then broke free and were chased seven blocks to the chain-link fence that separates the speeding traffic of the Belt Parkway from the residential streets.

There, among the weeds, bushes and broken bottles, the two men were beaten mercilessly. In terror, Griffith dove through a hole in the fence and tried to cross the highway. He was struck by a car, his body hurled against the divider. He died instantly. The driver, a white man, kept going. Later he told authorities he thought he'd struck an animal.

Dorr stared at me, then grinned. "They really fucked that eggplant up, right?" he said.

By then, I'd heard that hateful rant so many times that I felt unclean. I despaired of our leadership, our determination to see justice done, our great uncaring middle class so self-absorbed and complacent. In some ways, my journey had been a circle. The "answers" I'd been seeking were obvious.

Of course the Dragons were out there. They dwelt on the dark side of our hearts.